Cambridge Elements ≡

Elements in Religion and Violence
edited by
James R. Lewis
Wuhan University
Margo Kitts
Hawai'i Pacific University

JUDAISM AND VIOLENCE

A Historical Analysis with Insights from Social Psychology

Robert Eisen

George Washington University

CAMBRIDGE
UNIVERSITY PRESS

CAMBRIDGE
UNIVERSITY PRESS

University Printing House, Cambridge CB2 8BS, United Kingdom

One Liberty Plaza, 20th Floor, New York, NY 10006, USA

477 Williamstown Road, Port Melbourne, VIC 3207, Australia

314–321, 3rd Floor, Plot 3, Splendor Forum, Jasola District Centre,
New Delhi – 110025, India

103 Penang Road, #05–06/07, Visioncrest Commercial, Singapore 238467

Cambridge University Press is part of the University of Cambridge.

It furthers the University's mission by disseminating knowledge in the pursuit of
education, learning, and research at the highest international levels of excellence.

www.cambridge.org
Information on this title: www.cambridge.org/9781108940672
DOI: 10.1017/9781108935388

First published 2021

A catalogue record for this publication is available from the British Library.

ISBN 978-1-108-94067-2 Paperback
ISSN 2397-9496 (online)
ISSN 2514-3786 (print)

Judaism and Violence

A Historical Analysis with Insights from Social Psychology

Elements in Religion and Violence

DOI: 10.1017/9781108935388

First published online: September 2021

Robert Eisen

George Washington University

Author for correspondence: Robert Eisen, eisen@gwu.edu

ABSTRACT: This Element explores the potential in Judaism to incite Jews to engage in violence against non-Jews. The analysis proceeds in historical fashion, with sections devoted to the Hebrew Bible, rabbinic Judaism, medieval and early modern Judaism, and modern Zionism. The last topic is given special attention because of its relevance to the current Middle East conflict. This Element also draws on insights from social psychology to explain Jewish violence –particularly, Social Identity Theory.

KEYWORDS: judaism, violence, zionism, social identity theory, religion

ISBNs: 9781108940672 (PB), 9781108935388 (OC)

ISSNs: 2397-9496 (online), 2514-3786 (print)

Contents

1 Introduction   1

2 The Hebrew Bible   8

3 Rabbinic Judaism   25

4 Medieval and Early Modern Judaism   38

5 Modern Zionism   44

6 Conclusions   67

References   78

1 Introduction

Since the creation of the state of Israel in 1948, the relationship between Judaism and violence has been a matter of international significance. Prior to this event, few would have predicted that Jewish views on violence – or any other issue, for that matter – would become so important; there are, after all, only 14.5 million Jews in the world, and they make up no more than 0.2 percent of the global population. Yet the establishment of Israel has thrust the issue of Judaism and violence into the spotlight. This event has resulted in a violent conflict in the Middle East that has had far-reaching consequences in the international arena, and thus Jewish views on violence have become highly consequential for the world in general.

The Middle East conflict is, of course, first and foremost a conflict between Jews and Palestinians. Jews see the establishment of the state of Israel as a triumphant return to their homeland after two thousand years of exile in which they were a subjugated and persecuted minority in Europe and in the Islamic world. Palestinians see the same event as an unmitigated disaster that dispossessed them of their land by foreign invaders and has caused them deep suffering ever since.

The conflict, however, is so much more. It pits Israel not just against Palestinians but also against the Arab and Muslim worlds, and while at the time of this writing relations between Israel and its Arab neighbors seem better than they have at any time in the past, a comprehensive peace in the Middle East is still far off. Even more important, the Middle East conflict has become the focus of much larger tensions in the international arena between the Western world that has supported Israel – especially the United States – and the Arab and Muslims worlds that have supported the Palestinians. The West views Israel as an ally and a bastion of democracy in the Middle East that the Arab and Muslim worlds would do well to emulate, while Arabs and Muslims view the establishment of Israel as an attempt on the part of the West to dominate their worlds as it has done in the past. These tensions have never resulted in outright war. These parties have never fought a war solely over Israel. Nonetheless, tensions over Israel have certainly factored into the wars that the West has fought in recent decades in Iraq and Afghanistan; radical Islamist ideologues who have been active in these wars view their conflict with the West through the prism of a worldview in which Israel and the West have conspired to destroy the Islamic world. The 9/11 attacks were also justified by radical Muslims in light of this world-view. The Middle East conflict is therefore not confined to the Middle East; it involves the entire relationship between the Western world and the Arab and Muslim worlds, and it thus constitutes one of the greatest threats to world peace.

Against this background, it should be clear why the attitudes of Jews to violence have become a matter of such importance in the international sphere. Strange as it may seem, the views of this tiny people on this one issue have ramifications not just for the stability of the Middle East but for the stability of the world as a whole.

This Element is devoted to providing insight into these views. Its purpose is to examine the dimensions of Judaism that can inspire violence among its adherents. My focus will not be entirely on the Middle East conflict. Jews have reflected on the issue of violence throughout their history, which has spanned at least three thousand years. The Hebrew Bible, which evolved during the first millennium BCE, contains a good deal of material on violence, and Jews reflected on this material during subsequent centuries when they had no political power. My analysis of violence in Judaism will therefore grapple with the Bible and its later Jewish interpreters. However, given the importance of the Middle East conflict in our time, much of my effort will be invested in explaining how Jewish views on violence have played a part in this conflict. This focus also makes sense in light of the fact that the creation of the state of Israel has inspired Jews to engage in discussions about violence that are far more extensive and far richer than any conducted since the loss of their political independence two thousand years ago.

There are, of course, elements in Judaism that serve to restrain violence or that go further in encouraging peace. In fact, there are just as many elements of this kind in Judaism as there are those that encourage violence. As I have shown in a previous book, one can find sources on both sides of this divide in every major school of thought in Judaism from the Bible to modern Zionism (Eisen, 2011). However, the focus here will be solely on the violent dimension of Judaism.

By focusing exclusively on this side of Judaism, I am in no way implying that Judaism is inherently violent nor that Judaism is more violent that other religions. If, as I have just stated, Judaism has both violent and peaceful elements within it, Judaism can be violent, or peaceful, depending on which dimension its adherents choose to accentuate. However, I believe that it is valuable – in fact, imperative – to explore the violent dimension of Judaism in its own right. First, such an exploration will provide critical insight for resolving the Middle East conflict. What I hope to show in this Element is that, when Judaism has become violent, it has usually been for understandable reasons, and this is very much the case with the Middle East conflict. Thus, anyone interested in resolving the Middle East conflict must be aware of this background. If one understands why Jews have entered the conflict, one will be much better equipped to convince them to exit it. Effective conflict resolution must always begin with in-depth conflict analysis. I also believe that exploring Judaism's violent dimension is valuable for Jews themselves quite apart from events in the Middle East. Jews cannot create an authentic Judaism for the modern age without acknowledging and understanding Judaism's violent side. That goes even for Jews who favor a peaceful reading of Judaism – and I happen to be one of those Jews. They too must grapple with Judaism's darker side, even if they choose to reject it.

Everything I am saying here applies not just to Judaism but to all major religions. All of them have a violent and a peaceful dimension; all of them can become violent or peaceful in practice depending on which dimension their adherents emphasize; and adherents of these religions must acknowledge and grapple with their violent elements, even if they prefer the elements in them that are peaceful (Appleby, 2000).

A number of other caveats are in order regarding this study. If it is not already obvious, my focus in this Element will be exclusively on how Judaism treats violence perpetrated by Jews against non-Jews. There are, of course, other types of violence that are pertinent to Judaism, such as violence against women, gays, and heretics. We also have plenty of instances in Jewish texts that depict God's violent behavior toward human beings, both Jews and non-Jews. Yet, while these issues are worthy of treatment, they pale in importance in today's world to Jewish violence toward non-Jews because of the significance of the Middle East conflict in international affairs. My interest will therefore be solely on violence of this kind.

I must also emphasize that, while the Middle East conflict will be central to this Element, I will be making no moral judgments about it. My sole interest here is in understanding the potential for Judaism to foment violence and how that potential is triggered into action. Any moral judgments about Zionism – or Judaism as a whole, for that matter – would require a separate discussion. Therefore, I will make no attempt to determine whether Jews have been justified in creating the state of Israel, nor will I take any position on the justice of Israel's actions, once it came into existence. In Section 5 on Zionism, my concern will be to determine why Jews have made use of violence in the modern era in order to build their own state and what connection that violence has with Judaism.

Finally, I should note that this is my third book-length project on Judaism and violence, and it covers ground similar to that dealt with in *The Peace and Violence of Judaism: From the Bible to Modern Zionism* (Eisen, 2011). However, this Element differs from that book in a number of respects. First, it is shorter and more introductory in nature, given the intent of Cambridge's Elements series of which it is a part. Second, it tackles the question of Judaism and violence with new emphases. It is more historical in orientation than my previous book. It also makes use of insights from social psychology – in particular, Social Identity Theory – a field that was mentioned in my previous book but was not as central to my deliberations as it is in this Element.

1.1 Defining Violence

The term "violence" has been defined in several ways, and it is therefore important that I say something about how I understand the term. The definition provided by the World Health Organization (WHO) will suffice for my purposes. According to this definition, violence is "the intentional use of physical force or power, threatened or actual, against oneself, another person, or against a group or community, that either results in or has the high likelihood of resulting in injury, death, psychological harm, maldevelopment, or deprivation" (Krug et al., 2002: 5). Note that there are three categories of violence here: self-inflicted, interpersonal, and collective. I will be interested in the third category. That is, I will be looking at Jewish views on violence toward other people.

The WHO definition of violence also describes those actions that constitute violence. Primary among them are those that result in physical harm or death. When people speak about violence, they usually have this type of action in mind. However, included in the definition are other forms of injury. Thus, mention is made of actions that result in, or are likely to result in, "psychological damage." That is, the mere threat of violence or verbal abuse of other kinds may be considered violence if it has a markedly deleterious psychological impact on the victim. Symbolic injury, such as the desecration of objects or places sacred to a particular religious group, may constitute violence for the same reason. Scholars also extend the definition of violence to what is often referred to as "structural violence," a category not clearly represented in the WHO definition. This type of violence involves one group oppressing another politically, socially, or economically so that the subjugated group suffers physically and psychologically over a lengthy period of time. Thus, even if blood is not spilled in such situations, the damage done over the long term can be just as harmful as more direct physical injury, and it is therefore often classified as violence (Galtung, 1990).

My study will focus primarily on the kind of violence that causes physical injury or death, particularly when it is perpetrated on a mass scale. War is the best example of this type of violence. However, I will also have occasion to refer to structural violence in my discussion of the Middle East conflict.

It is common to differentiate between violence that is unprovoked and aggressive and violence that is defensive, and it is also common to condemn the first type of violence and approve of the second. I will bring this distinction into my deliberations in the coming pages, but I will do so with great caution because it can be very difficult to differentiate between the two categories of violence. An individual or a group may act violently with the claim that they are only defending themselves, when, in truth, their actions are aggressive. Even terrorist groups often claim that their violence is only for defensive purposes.

1.2 Methodology

My method in this Element will be primarily historical. I will trace the evolution of Jewish attitudes to violence throughout history. Sections will be devoted to the Hebrew Bible, rabbinic Judaism, medieval and early modern Judaism, and modern Zionism. A concluding section will then sum up my thoughts in the preceding sections and share some speculations about the future.

My analysis will assume that two main factors determine whether or not a people will engage in violence. The first is culture, which defines the attitudes and practices by which the constituents of a society relate to each other and to the world around them. Social scientists have done a great deal of work on the relationship between culture and violence, and they have discovered that cultures have widely different approaches to this issue (Ross, 1993). Those differences can usually be explained by past experiences. For instance, a people that has endured multiple traumas is likely to have a culture that is more prone to violence than one that has not (Volkan, 2007). The second major factor determining whether a people will engage in violence is historical context. Just because a culture has features that make it prone to violence does not mean that it will necessarily act in a violent manner in a given situation. It will become violent only when the right historical circumstances trigger its violent tendencies.

With regard to Judaism, my thesis will be that Jews developed a culture capable of violence against outsiders during the period of the Hebrew Bible and early rabbinic Judaism, a period that spanned more than two thousand years, from approximately 1500 BCE to 750 CE. During this lengthy stretch of time, Jews experienced a series of traumas that shaped the way they understood history and their role in it from a theological standpoint, and that theology of history contained within it the potential to inspire Jews to violence. It saw the Jews as God's chosen people who, despite whatever defeats they experienced, would eventually triumph in the messianic period. All that was needed to bring the violent potential in this theology into action were the right historical circumstances. Those circumstances arose period-ically during the biblical and early rabbinic periods, but after the Jews lost their political sovereignty in the first century, it would be many centuries before circumstances were ripe again for Jews to engage in violence. Those circumstances eventually came about with the advent of the Zionist move-ment and the drama surrounding the creation of the state of Israel. These events heralded the return of Jewish violence to the world stage.

If, as I am claiming here, Jewish violence in the modern period is the result of a culture shaped by past traumas, mention has to be made of the Holocaust. Many mistakenly assume that this trauma inspired Jews to build a modern Jewish state and engage in violence for that purpose. The death of 6 million Jews during the Second World War was certainly a major catastrophe for Jews, and it was undoubtedly an important factor in motivating Jews to create the state of Israel. However, too much attention has been paid to the Holocaust in explaining Jewish violence in the Middle East. The beginning of the Zionist movement predated the Holocaust by sixty years and was inspired by the centuries of Jewish suffering long before this event. In fact, Jews were the victims of violence in one form or another from biblical times onward. Moreover, violence by Jews against their Arab enemies predated the Holocaust as well. Jewish settlers in Palestine were involved in violent confrontations with Palestinians not long after they established the first Jewish settlements there. Thus, the desire of Jews to establish their own state and their capacity to engage in violence for that purpose cannot be attributed to the Holocaust alone.

My analysis in this Element will be enriched by insights that I plan to bring in from the social sciences. I have already noted the important work done by social scientists on the relationship between culture and violence, but my interest in the social sciences will be focused primarily on one particular school of social psychology that has carried out very valuable work on violence in recent years: Social Identity Theory (henceforth, SIT). This school explores the ubiquitous tendency of human beings to join groups and identify with their agenda, and, in doing so, it also provides important insights into the capacity for groups to engage in violence. I believe the insights of SIT into violence can be applied to modern Jews as well. My analysis here will also benefit from another series of insights in the social sciences that belong to Vamik Volkan, a psychoanalyst who has written extensively on ethnic violence in the past thirty years.

It may seem odd that I would use the insights of social psychology to analyze events that date back to the biblical and rabbinic periods, seeing as those insights are predicated on data gleaned from ethnic and national conflicts that have taken place in just the last thirty to forty years. However, such insights have proven to be highly valuable in improving our understanding of the violent tendencies in a wide variety of cultures in our contemporary world, and I therefore believe that they are of value for understanding cultures that long predate this world as well. My sense is that they reveal truths about fundamental aspects of human nature and its capacity for violence, truths that are applicable in all places and times. We therefore have much to gain by applying the insights of social psychology not just to events involving Jews in today's world but also to events they experienced long ago.

2 The Hebrew Bible

Our first task is to lay out the theology of history that emerges in the Hebrew Bible and rabbinic Judaism and to explore its potential for encouraging violence. This section will be devoted to the Hebrew Bible, while the next will focus on rabbinic Judaism.[1]

The Hebrew Bible presents us with unique challenges. It consists of an enormous amount of material that was composed during the first millennium BCE by authors who are mostly unidentifiable. The material is also highly heterogeneous; it includes narrative, law, and poetry, to name just a few of its genres. As a result, the Bible does not provide consistent positions on most of the topics it treats. However, coherent themes and ideas can still be discerned in its pages, and fortunately that is the case with

---

[1] I will be using the terms "Hebrew Bible" and "Bible" interchangeably in this section. While in Western scholarship the term "Bible" includes the New Testament, here it will refer only to the Hebrew Bible, or *Tanakh*, the biblical text recognized as canonical by Jews.

its theology of history; it is presented in a consistent enough fashion in the biblical text for us to describe its general contours.

One way to analyze the Bible's theology of history is to trace its evolution through various layers of the biblical text, but that exercise is one I will not attempt here. Biblical scholars have expended enormous energy just identifying and dating these layers even before analyzing their content, and there is still much disagreement over the conclusions to be drawn from these efforts. I cannot wade into these waters. It will be much more fruitful for my purposes to treat the Bible as a unified piece of literature and to describe the theology of history that its final editors wanted its readers to understand.[2] This approach to the Bible will not only avoid needless complexity; it is closest to the one that Jews themselves have taken toward the Bible throughout the centuries, and it is therefore the best way to help us understand why the biblical text has also been a source of violence for Jews. However, I will not entirely ignore the work of modern biblical scholars who attempt to parse the biblical text into layers and order them chronologically. This scholarship will be valuable for providing insights into the sections of the Bible most important for our topic.

2.1 The Covenant

The key notion in the Bible's theology of history is covenant. It is this concept that undergirds the entire relationship between God and the Israelites as it is depicted in the biblical text. The covenant idea has its roots in ancient Near Eastern culture. A covenant was, in essence, a contract between two parties, usually between a king and his vassals, in which each party had obligations to the other (Hillers, 1969). It was more than just a formal agreement, however; it assumed a deep sense of loyalty and trust between the parties.

The covenant between God and the Israelites in the Bible is modeled on this type of contract, and it begins to take shape in chapter 12 of Genesis

---

[2] Among academic approaches to the Bible, this approach is most similar to that of Brevard Childs who championed canonical criticism. However, while Childs assumed that the biblical canon included the New Testament, I will be focusing only on the Hebrew Bible.

when God first communicates with Abraham (Gen. 12:1–3). In this chapter, God informs Abraham that he is to be the forefather of a great nation and that this nation will be a source of blessing for all other nations. God's relationship with Abraham and his descendants is then concretized in a formal covenant ceremony in Genesis 15. This chapter also begins to spell out the basic terms of the covenantal agreement that will be elaborated upon in subsequent chapters in Genesis. The picture that soon emerges is that the covenant will require Abraham and his descendants to obey God, and God, in turn, will be obligated to reward them with material wealth and prosperity (Gen. 18:19, 22:17).

Key to this agreement is the land of Canaan, which will later be designated as "the land of Israel" (Gen. 12:7). The material blessing that Abraham's descendants will experience will take place in this land that God has given them as part of the covenant. In other words, the chosen people will have a chosen land. However, neither Abraham nor his descendants will take possession of the land immediately. Abraham is informed in the covenant ceremony in Genesis 15 that his descendants will first become slaves in Egypt for several hundred years. God will then redeem them, and they will go on to take possession of the land by conquering the Canaanite nations who inhabit it (Gen. 15:7–21).

Critical details about the covenant are not defined in Genesis, but they emerge later on in the Torah. An important question is what prescriptions God wants the Israelites to fulfill in order to demonstrate their obedience to him. That question is answered in several sections of the Torah in which God imparts scores of commandments to the Israelites. The first of these commandments are given to Moses, the chief Israelite prophet, in a spectacular revelation on Mount Sinai described in the book of Exodus (Ex. 20). However, the vast majority of the commandments appear in subsequent sections of the Torah. Some of the commandments prescribe a series of rituals that the Israelites will observe to worship God, the most prominent of which are animal sacrifices. Other commandments prescribe a series of ethical imperatives on the presumption that obedience to God requires the Israelites to create a just society.

Portions of the Torah also spell out the punishments the Israelites will incur if they do not adhere to these commandments. God informs them that they will no longer experience material prosperity, and if their disobedience continues, their enemies will conquer them and exile them from their land. In some passages, this threat is accompanied by a prediction that the Israelites will indeed merit this punishment later in their history. God promises, however, that his covenant with the Israelites will never be broken and that, even if the Israelites are exiled, he will eventually bring them back to their homeland (Lev. 22:14–46; Deut. 28:15–69).

In the books of the Prophets, the next major section of the Bible after the Torah, we are told that this redemption will inaugurate a utopian period that will be everlasting. The dynasty of King David – Israel's greatest king – will be restored, all nations will recognize the God of Israel as the one true God, and they will live in peace with each other (e.g., Isa. 40–66; Jer. 52; Ezek. 40–48). Similar predictions are found in other biblical books, such as the book of Daniel that is in the third section of the Hebrew Bible, known as the Writings (Dan. 7–12). These forecasts of a future utopia become the basis of the notion of the messianic period in later Judaism.

A question that is never clearly answered in the biblical text is why God needed to forge a covenantal relationship with the Israelites in the first place. This initiative seems to have been inspired by God's expectations of human beings from the beginning of creation and his frustration that they are unable to live up to them. When God creates the first humans, Adam and Eve, he places them in a paradise, the Garden of Eden, and he issues only one commandment to them: not to eat the fruit of the Tree of Knowledge of Good and Evil. Yet it is one commandment too many; they partake of the fruit and are punished by being exiled from the garden (Gen. 2–3). Ten generations later, when human beings have multiplied and populated the earth, they become so corrupt that God resorts to wiping out all of humanity in a flood and starting from scratch with Noah and his family who are deemed to be the only ones worthy of being rescued from the catastrophe (Gen. 6:9–10:32). Ten more generations later, when the human race has again multiplied and filled the earth, the wickedness of human beings again emerges; they band together to build an enormous tower in an apparent attempt to rebel against God. God responds by destroying the tower and dividing human beings into nations that speak different languages, with the apparent goal of not allowing them to work together ever again to rebel against him (Gen. 11:1–9). It is at this point that Abraham is summoned by God.

Thus, when God initiates a relationship with Abraham, it seems to represent a change in strategy on God's part regarding the human race. Having failed to secure obedience from human beings in general, God now focuses on cultivating obedience among one people, and one people alone, and it is for this reason that the covenant is needed; it is meant to define the relationship that God has with his chosen people so that they will fulfill their assigned role and receive God's blessing.

Yet the other nations of the world are not forgotten here; as we are told in Genesis 12, God's wish is that they too will share in the blessing promised to Abraham's descendants (Gen. 12:3). The biblical text never clarifies how the blessing will be imparted to the other nations, but, as noted, the Prophets speak about an idyllic age at some future time in which all nations will recognize the one true God and will forever live in peace with each other. Thus, at the very least, the nations of the world will experience God's blessing at this point in time (Niditch, 1993: 134; Greenberg, 1995: 388–90).

2.2 The Covenant in Biblical History

Thus far, we have looked at the theology of history in the Hebrew Bible as a theoretical construct. How, according to the Bible, does that construct work out in reality? As the events of the biblical history unfold from the time of Abraham onward, it becomes clear that God's scheme is fraught with challenges for much the same reason that God's initial scheme ran into difficulty in the first chapters of Genesis: human beings have a propensity to resist obedience to God, and the Israelites are prone to doing so as well. When the Israelites become settled in their land, they constantly succumb to the seduction of other gods and worship them, and as a result they eventually experience the worst of the punishments that God threatened to bring upon them; they are eventually conquered and exiled by their enemies.

The exile occurs in two stages. The first is at the hands of the Assyrian Empire. By the eighth century BCE, the Israelite kingdom had split into two – the northern kingdom that retained the title "Israel" and the southern kingdom of "Judah," named after the largest of the tribes that resided therein. The Assyrians conquer the kingdom of Israel in 722 BCE and exile its inhabitants to a number of different locations. These Israelites are never heard from again in the biblical text (2 Kings 17:1–6). The southern kingdom of Judah manages to avoid the same fate; but, in the next century, the Babylonian Empire becomes the major threat in the region and, in 587 BCE, they conquer Judah and destroy the Temple in Jerusalem that was Judaism's central shrine and the location in which animal sacrifices were performed to worship God. The Babylonians also exile most of the Judeans to Babylonia (2 Kings 25). Yet God's promise that the covenant will never be broken appears to be upheld when the Persian Empire destroys the Babylonian Empire and becomes the next major power in the region. The Persians now rule over the community of exiled Judeans in Babylonia, and their emperor, Cyrus, allows them to return to their homeland to rebuild their state and their Temple in Jerusalem (Ezra 1). This marks the beginning of an era referred to by scholars as the "Second Temple period" in Jewish history, and it will last several hundred years. It is also at this point in history that historians refer to the Judeans as "Jews" and to the religion they observe as "Judaism." However, the state the Jews rebuild is much diminished compared to the first one, and the Jews remain under Persian domination.

It is here that the biblical account of history comes to an end. Thus, by the end of the historical narrative in the Bible, the expectation of a utopian future era remains unfulfilled. Neither are the Jews sovereign in their land under a restored Davidic dynasty nor is the world at peace, as the Prophets had predicted.

Despite this inconclusive ending, the basic features of the Bible's theology of history are clear; history begins with creation and will end with a utopian world that resembles the paradise with which human history began. Between these poles, history is characterized by the story of how human beings struggle to become worthy of God's blessing. Abraham's descendants play a key role in this process; they are meant to be role models for the rest of the nations in their relationship with God. However, they have great difficulty living up to this expectation, and the Bible concludes with that struggle still in progress.

2.3 Violence

Let us now focus on the issue of greatest concern to us, which is the violence inflicted by the Israelites and Judeans on other nations. Violence of this kind occurs throughout the biblical history. The most salient instance is the violence perpetrated by the Israelites against the Canaanite nations whose land they conquer as part of their covenantal agreement with God. The Israelites are commanded by God not just to take possession of the land but to annihilate its inhabitants – men, women, and children. The reason given in the biblical text for this imperative is that God does not want the Israelites to come into contact with Canaanite idolatry lest they abandon him and worship Canaanite gods (Deut. 7:2–4, 20:16–18).

Another nation that is supposed to meet a fate similar to that of the Canaanites is Amalek. We are told in the book of Exodus that, just after the Israelites are redeemed from Egypt, they are attacked by the Amalekites. The Israelites prevail in the ensuing battle, but God commands them to continue their war against the Amalekites in the future and to annihilate them, the assumption being that the Amalekites who attacked the Israelites were part of a much larger people. The war with the Amalekites is couched in cosmic terms; God himself will be at war with the Amalekites throughout the ages (Ex. 17:8–16). Another account of this episode in Deuteronomy explains that the punishment of the Amalekites is due to the fact that they were merciless in waging war against a weary and beleaguered nation that had just escaped centuries of slavery (Deut. 25:17–19). It is not clear from the biblical text if the commandment to annihilate the Amalekites is ever entirely fulfilled. The Amalekites appear periodically in the biblical history after the Israelites become settled in their land, and the Israelites sometimes wage war on them (e.g., 1 Sam. 15), but they are not heard from after the reign of King David (2 Sam. 1:12). Yet, whatever the outcome here, the intent of God's command is clear enough; the Amalekites must be wiped out – men, women, and children – just as the Canaanites had been.

Also significant for our purposes is the violence reported in the Bible that will precede the utopian period that God promises will come into existence at some future point in time. As noted, the biblical narrative predicts that the Israelites will be exiled for their sins but that they will return to their land under a reconstituted Davidic monarchy. In this period, they will enjoy prosperity, and the nations of the world will live in everlasting peace and recognize the God of Israel. Yet, in numerous biblical passages, we are also told that, before this era begins, God will go to war on the nations who have oppressed the Israelites (Isa. 63:2–5; Zech. 9). Some of these passages are directed specifically at the Edomites, a nation that neighbored the Israelite kingdom and was their longtime enemy (Isa. 34–35; Ezek. 25:12–14; Obad. 1).

2.4 Insights from Biblical Scholarship

Biblical scholars have done a great deal of work to illuminate the background of the texts we have described up to this point. The story about the Canaanite genocide seems to have been composed in the seventh century BCE when the Assyrians had destroyed the northern kingdom of Israel and was now a threat to the southern kingdom of Judah. During this period, King Josiah came to power in Judah and seems to have believed that the Judeans could defend themselves against the Assyrians only if they secured God's help. However, the Judeans at the time were also worshipping other deities, and Josiah therefore instituted a reform program that purged Judean culture of its foreign gods and enjoined Judeans to worship God alone. This program marked an important development in ancient Israelite religion because it introduced a purer monotheism than the Israelites or the Judeans had known up to that time. This brand of monotheism would continue to develop over the next century when the Judeans went into exile, and it would become one of the most defining features of Judaism as it took shape in the postexilic period (Smith, 2001: 165–66; Tigay, 2003: 433).

Yet more important for our purposes is that, according to biblical scholars, Josiah's religious reform was supported by Judean historians who began composing a history of Israel when the reform was instituted, a history that was refined over the next century. The result was a work that encompassed the book of Deuteronomy in the Torah and all the historical books of the Prophets from Joshua to the end of 2 Kings. The major theme of this work was that the Israelites had been able to vanquish their foes and remain secure in their land as long as they worshipped the one true God.

The lesson that the historians apparently hoped to teach the Judeans was that they too could be victorious against their idolatrous Assyrian enemies if they maintained the same monotheistic faith their ancestors had. The story about the conquest of the Canaanites that appeared in the book of Joshua was central to this agenda. Its message was that the Israelites had been able to take possession of the land God had promised them because of their faith in him, a faith that was juxtaposed against the idolatry of the land's former inhabitants (Niditch, 1993: 74–77).

The Canaanite genocide was therefore a fiction that served a valuable political function. Scholars have proposed that the story may have been based on tensions between Israelite and Canaanite communities earlier in history, but the genocide that it describes was imagined. Supporting this conclusion is the fact that archeologists have found no evidence of a genocidal destruction in the layers of archeological excavations in Israel that should have brought forth such evidence (Rowlett, 1996: Kaminsky, 2007: 113–14).

Scholars and thinkers have sometimes taken comfort in these conclusions on the assumption that, if the Canaanite genocide never happened, one need not see it as morally problematic. However, as we will soon see, that is faulty reasoning. Even if the Canaanite conquest is fictional, it is treated as genuine history in the biblical text, generations of Jews and Christians would understand it in that manner, and some of them would use it to justify violence against their enemies (Eisen, 2011: 27).

With regard to the Amalekites, one can draw conclusions similar to those regarding the Canaanite genocide. The Amalekites seem to have been a real people who were enemies of the Israelites, but there is no hard evidence that the Israelites annihilated them.[3] Nonetheless, here too the Bible treats the imperative to wipe out the Amalekites as accurate history, and this too is morally problematic (Eisen, 2011: 28–29).

Biblical scholars also have much to tell us about the violence that several passages in the biblical text predict will accompany the arrival of the future

---

[3] The specter of Amalek appears to persist in the person of Haman the Agagite in the book of Esther. Haman is presumably descended from Agag, the Amalekite king whose death is described in 1 Samuel.

utopia. These predictions are found most frequently in the books of the Prophets that were composed from the eighth to the sixth centuries BCE. They are also found in others biblical books, most notably Daniel 7–12 that dates to the second century BCE.

Here too, it would seem, the inspiration to compose such texts came from outside threats. The prophetic texts were written against the backdrop of the same situation that produced the Deuteronomic History. As we already know, the period of the eighth to the sixth centuries BCE in which these texts were composed was one in which the kingdoms of Israel and Judah were being threatened by the Assyrian and Babylonian empires. Daniel 7–12 was written under similar circumstances. The book of Daniel presents itself as a text written by a Judean figure who lived during the period of the Babylonian exile in the sixth century BCE, but scholars have shown that chapters 7–12 actually date to the second century BCE when the Jews were ruled by the Greek Seleucid monarchs who inherited a portion of Alexander the Great's empire. The book appears to have been a reaction to events in the time of one of these monarchs in particular, Antiochus Epiphanes IV, whose decrees threatened traditional Jewish worship in Jerusalem and ignited a civil war (Wills, 2014: 1636). The intent of the predictions in all these books is clear; they were inspired by a desire for revenge against the nations that had done violence to the Israelites and Judeans.

What emerges here is that the passages depicting the worst instances of Israelite and Judean violence in the Hebrew Bible were, in fact, the product of violence of which the Israelites and Judeans were themselves victims. The violence that empires inflicted upon the Israelites and Judeans inspired them to imagine themselves as perpetrators of violence at both the beginning of their history and its end. The violence of the Assyrian Empire in the eighth century BCE inspired the story of the Canaanite genocide that was purported to have occurred centuries earlier, and its purpose was to bolster the courage of Judeans in the face of the Assyrian threat. The violence of the Assyrian and Babylonian empires also motivated the Prophets to predict violence against these nations and other enemies of Israel in the future utopia, and here the intent was to assure the Israelites and Judeans that, whatever victories their enemies achieved, they would eventually be punished. The author of Daniel 7–12 did something similar in light of Antiochus's persecution. In short, the need on the part of the Israelites and Judeans to engage in violence for defensive reasons ended up spinning off fantasies of violence that was aggressive in nature both in the imagined past and in the imagined future.

None of these imagined events had to spawn actual aggressive violence on the part of the later generations of Jews who believed in them. By the time the stories about the Canaanites and Amalekites became part of Israel's sacred literature, they described events that had supposedly happened long ago in its history. As for the violence that was supposed to precede the future utopia, the biblical text usually describes this violence as being inflicted on the nations directly by God. The job of the Israelites and Judeans is to observe God's commandments so that he will reward them by vanquishing their foes and sending them back to their homeland.

However, one can easily see how these imagined events had the potential to lead Jews to violence. If Jews believed that God issued orders in the past to annihilate such wicked nations as the Canaanites and Amalekites, perhaps the lesson here was that Jews should take the initiative to do the same with other wicked nations even in the absence of an explicit command. This argument would be strengthened by the notion that the wicked nations of the world had to be vanquished before Jews could experience the future utopia predicted by the Prophets. Thus, there was an inherent ambiguity in the message that Jews could glean from the imagined events examined here, and as we will see in the next section, Jews grappled with that ambiguity later on in their history.

It is also important to note that not all of the mass violence perpetrated by the Israelites in the Hebrew Bible was imagined. The biblical text reports on numerous wars waged by the Israelites against their neighbors, and these wars may reflect actual historical events. Moreover, many of them were not defensive in nature. For instance, most of 2 Samuel is devoted to King David's reign, and the narrative describes David's numerous military initiatives. While these initiatives are almost always taken against Israel's enemies, it is not clear from the biblical text that they are consistently in response to an immediate threat (e.g., 2 Sam. 8). These wars are less central to our concerns because they were never viewed as having the same importance in the biblical-rabbinic theology of history as those already discussed in this section. However, they had the potential to inspire Jews to look at violence favorably, and, as we will see, that is precisely the effect they had on some Zionists in the modern period.

Also important in this regard are the books of 1–2 Maccabees that depict Jews engaging in violence in the revolt against Antiochus Epiphanes IV. These texts were not included in the Jewish biblical canon, and therefore, by the rabbinic period, they would no longer be familiar to most Jews. The rabbis would commemorate the Jewish victory over Antiochus and his forces in the holiday of Hanukkah, but without a focus on the violence perpetrated in that victory (Babylonian Talmud, *Shabbat* 21b). Yet the same secular Zionists who looked to the Bible as inspiration for violence would resurrect the books of Maccabees for the same purpose.

2.5 Social Identity Theory

I said in my introductory section that recent advances in social psychology would help illuminate the issues covered in this book, particularly those found in Social Identity Theory (SIT), and I believe that this is the case with the material in the Hebrew Bible discussed here.

Let us begin with a quick summary of the major points of SIT. This branch of psychology examines the ubiquitous tendency among human beings to join groups and identify with their agenda. According to SIT, this tendency is natural because belonging to a group enhances an individual's sense of self-esteem. The kinds of groups that individuals usually identify with are ethnic or national groups, but the proponents of SIT have discovered that individuals will gravitate toward groups on the basis of even the most minimal and superficial markers of distinction. Moreover, one can belong to more than one group at a time. Thus, one may have both an ethnic identity and a national identity, even though the constituents of the two groups will not be the same (Hogg, 2016; Demmers, 2017: 42–47).

A feature of SIT most relevant to our concerns is that social identity can often be the cause of violent conflict because identifying with a particular group is usually accompanied by an automatic and unconscious impulse to believe in the superiority of one's own group over others. This tendency is especially strong when a group is under stress for any reason – political, economic, or social. In such situations, the group will not only insist on its own superiority over other groups; it will demonize other groups by ascribing to them negative attributes that do not necessarily have a basis in reality. Moreover, the outside groups being demonized may have nothing to do with the stresses the demonizing group is experiencing. The outside groups serve as scapegoats for the demonizing group's problems (Lüders et al., 2016).

In the past few years, proponents of SIT have begun to apply their insights to religion on the premise that religion is one of the most powerful, if not *the* most powerful, form of identity on both the individual and group level. Here, one's sense of self-esteem is determined by establishing a relationship with supernatural forces or beings mostly hidden from us that control our fortunes in this life and, in many instances, the afterlife as well. In addition, one's sense of self-esteem is enhanced by this relationship because religion usually involves belonging to an entire group of individuals who believe in the same supernatural forces or beings and the effects they have on human beings. Religion is therefore a powerful form of identity because the stakes are very high. By tying one's identity to forces or beings who are in control of one's fate and to an entire community that marks its identity in the same way, religious identity often becomes the most critical element in a person's sense of self (Seul, 1999: 558–63; Ysseldyk et al., 2010; Mavor & Ysseldyk, 2020).

Furthermore, if social identity tends to cause a group to feel superior to other groups, social identity predicated on religion will have an even stronger tendency to do so because, once again, the stakes are so high. The same can be said about the capacity for social identity to motivate groups under stress to engage in violence. If social identity is likely to cause a group to demonize other groups and act violently against them, social identity based on religion will accentuate that tendency because, again, so much is at stake (Seul, 1999: 563; Ysseldyk et al., 2010: 63–64).

These insights help explain central features of Judean religion and the religion of Judaism that would emerge from it. The Judeans were well aware of the fact that they were a small people, sandwiched between two large and powerful civilizations – Mesopotamia and Egypt – and that they were therefore vulnerable to attack on either side. That awareness comes through in numerous ways in the biblical literature that Judean culture would produce (Brett, 1995; 161–62; Kaminsky, 2007: 76–77; Eisen, 2011: 50–53). The worst of the Judeans' fears was initially realized in relation to empires in Mesopotamia. As we have seen, in the eighth century BCE, the Assyrians set their sights on the conquest of the northern kingdom of Israel and the southern kingdom of Judah and managed to destroy the former kingdom in 722 BCE. The southern kingdom was spared, but the Judeans were then confronted in the seventh century BCE with the Babylonians who conquered them and took them into exile. In the sixth century BCE, the Persians allowed the Judeans to return to their homeland, but they remained subjugated to Persian rule. From the fourth to the first centuries BCE, the Judeans confronted threats from outside Mesopotamia and Egypt. They were conquered by the Greeks and then the Romans, though the Judeans achieved a brief respite of independence between the two conquests when the Hasmonean kings ruled for about a century after the Maccabees defeated Antiochus and his forces.

According to SIT, the constituents of a group under threat will tend to accentuate their social identity, and the Judeans, who were under one threat or another for several centuries, did just that. In response to these threats, they constructed a social identity that was unusually strong, beginning with King Josiah's reforms that we have already described. Josiah's reform program spurred the construction of a social identity for the Judeans that was based on religion, which, as the proponents of SIT have noted, is a particularly potent form of social identity. Moreover, the religion fashioned in Josiah's program was predicated on the bold claim that a very powerful God had chosen the ancestors of the Judeans and their descendants as his beloved people. He would protect them as long as they obeyed his will, but even if they were disobedient, his love for them would always remain. In fact, according to Josiah's reforms, this God was the *only* God; there was no other. God ruled all the nations of the earth whether they knew it or not, and all the gods that these other nations believed in were mere chimeras (Smith, 2001: 165–66). One could hardly imagine a more robust form of social identity than this one. Josiah was staking the identity of the

Judeans on the existence of an all-powerful being who had exalted the Judeans above all other nations.

We must pause here to appreciate how extraordinary it was for a small kingdom like Judah to create this kind of identity. The Judeans were surrounded by far more powerful enemies, the strength of which belied their grandiose claims. In the situation that the Judeans were in, however, the identity instilled in them by Josiah's reforms was just what they needed. It helped them weather the Assyrian threat.

It did more than that, though. It also helped the Judeans deal with all the subsequent threats they would face for the next several centuries. The beliefs associated with the identity shaped by Josiah's reforms were consolidated during the period of the Babylonian exile and the return of the Judeans to their homeland, and they became central and permanent features of Judaism that helped the Judeans survive subsequent conquests. From an academic perspective, there was a good bit of luck involved in the survival of the Judeans. However, the Judeans did not see it this way. They believed that the God who was the universe's sole deity was on their side, and the fact that they managed to survive the many threats they faced seems to have reinforced these beliefs. In short, the precarious situation of the Judeans over several centuries required them to adopt a fierce sense of identity if they were going to have any chance of surviving the many threats they faced, and that identity was provided by Josiah's reform.

SIT also teaches us that, when a group feels threatened, its constituents will not only accentuate their identity; they will often demonize outside groups, even those that have nothing to do with the threats they face, and this process often sets the stage for violence. These tendencies are also in evidence in the biblical literature that came out of Josiah's reform program. For Josiah, violence seems to have been the intended outcome of the social identity he tried to construct. The Judeans had to defend themselves against the Assyrians, and therefore Josiah attempted to create a strong social identity based on monotheism that would inspire them to fight bravely against their more powerful opponents. Yet Josiah's program also resulted in the projection of violence against a third party that had purportedly lived long ago and had nothing to do with the Assyrians. The Deuteronomic historians composed a history reflecting Josiah's program in which the ancestors of the Judeans were depicted as taking possession of their land because of their faith in the one true God who commanded them to slaughter the nations who inhabited it. Thus, as SIT suggests, the pressures exerted on the Judeans prompted them to demonize a third party unrelated to those pressures and to commit acts of violence against them; however, in this case, the third party was the Canaanites who existed only in an imagined past. Still, the Judeans came to regard the genocidal campaign against the Canaanites as history, and therefore what began as a reform program to motivate the Judeans to use violence to defend themselves against their current enemies resulted in a story canonized in their sacred literature that celebrated the use of violence against nations in the past that was unprovoked.

SIT also helps explain the violence found in texts of the Bible that pertain to the future utopian period. Here too the violence is imagined but is the product of a simpler psychological mechanism than that involving the Canaanites. As noted in Section 2.4, this violence was simply a revenge fantasy against the nations that had acted violently against the Israelites and Judeans over a period of several centuries. Thus, here Israelite and Judean prophets asserted their social identity by predicting that, in the end, their people would triumph against their enemies.

I should clarify that none of the psychological processes that I have attributed to the Israelites and Judeans were necessarily conscious. Social identity theorists presume that such processes are the product of the subconscious. They are rooted in natural impulses hardwired into us by evolution. The problem here, of course, is that it is very difficult to prove anything about the subconscious realm. What is said about this dimension of human personalities will always be speculative, especially when we are dealing with people who lived thousands of years ago. Nonetheless, the insights of SIT are derived empirically through extensive data gleaned from surveys and experiments, and even though these data are concerned with modern human collectives, they have been confirmed across such a wide variety of groups that they seem to be telling us something valuable about attributes basic to human nature. For this reason, I believe that SIT has much to offer us in understanding the violence of the Bible.

An important corollary to these observations is that, if they are correct, the most vilified aspects of the Hebrew Bible are an expression of characteristics that are, in fact, found in all human groups. What SIT teaches us is that practically every human collective – be it ethnic, national, or religious – sees itself as "chosen" in some respect, even if it does not use that precise terminology (Eisen, 2011: 53). In fact, we have evidence that other nations in the ancient Near East besides the Israelites and Judeans also saw themselves as chosen (Cross, 1973: 105). SIT also shows that groups tend to view themselves as superior to other groups, and thus practically every group is capable of demonizing other groups and being violent toward them. Thus, the violence described in the sacred literature of the Israelites and Judeans should not be regarded as exceptional. This literature may have expressed the human tendencies examined in SIT in a particularly violent manner but that was only because the people who produced this literature experienced constant threats from outsiders that served to accentuate these tendencies.

2.6 Conclusions

To sum up our discussion, the constant pressures from outside threats that the Israelites and Judeans experienced in the biblical period prompted the Judeans to construct a religious identity based on remarkable claims. They may have been a small people in the ancient Near East surrounded by powerful empires, but they insisted that the one true God was *their* God, and he would protect them from their adversaries so long as they obeyed his will. These claims helped the Judeans survive the threats against them.

Most important for our concerns, such claims also prompted the Judeans to view violence in a positive manner. With the belief that God was on their side, they were emboldened to fight the Assyrian and Babylonian enemies who threatened them from the eighth to the sixth century BCE. This positive perspective on violence may be excused because it was a matter of self-defense. However, the threats that the Judeans had to deal with also prompted them to project a more aggressive type of violence onto the past with the claim that they had initially taken possession of their land through wars that were waged with God's help. Moreover, the Judeans – as well as the Israelites, in this instance – projected the same type of violence onto their future with the claim that the idyllic era predicted by the prophets would be ushered in by the violent punishment of the nations that had oppressed them – though here it would be God himself who would take the lead.

We also noted that the biblical text depicted the Israelite kings as waging unprovoked wars against their enemies, and these wars were likely to have reflected actual historical events. The same goes for the violence depicted in the extracanonical books 1 and 2 Maccabees. These wars, however, were not central to the theology of history as developed in the Hebrew Bible.

The important question for us is how the violent elements of the biblical text affected the behavior of Jews in subsequent centuries. We noted in Section 2.4 that the theology of history in the Bible did not have to inspire later generations of Jews to engage in aggressive forms of violence against their adversaries but that it certainly could. Much depended on the degree to which Jews were willing to adopt the positive views of violence of their ancestors and use them as inspiration for dealing with their own enemies. In the next section, we will see that, as the rabbinic period got underway, Jews were deeply divided on this issue.

3 Rabbinic Judaism

There is a common misperception in the Western world that Judaism is synonymous with the Hebrew Bible, and the reason for this is obvious. The religion most Westerners are familiar with is Christianity, which incorporated the Hebrew Bible into its own Scripture, and therefore the Hebrew Bible is the only Jewish text with which Westerners have acquaintance. As a result, Westerners are often unaware of the rich developments that Judaism underwent after the Hebrew Bible was canonized.

In fact, the religion we call Judaism is based as much on these later developments as it is on the Hebrew Bible. As the Hebrew Bible came into its final form around the second century CE, a new group of religious leaders known as "rabbis" began to emerge in the Jewish community, and by the beginning of the ninth century, they were its dominant leaders. The thinking of the rabbis was recorded in a large body of literature, but by far their most important work was the Talmud, a massive multivolume compendium of their discussions recorded over several centuries. The Talmud achieved its final form in Babylonia in the eighth century, and it soon became the most important work in Judaism after the Hebrew Bible. Thus, as of the ninth century, Judaism consisted of the Hebrew Bible as understood and interpreted by the rabbis.

The hegemony of the rabbis had remarkable longevity. Their Judaism was the Judaism of the vast majority of Jews until the nineteenth century. The authority of the rabbis began to break down in this period due to the momentous changes that the Jewish community in Europe was undergoing at this time. As democracy and natural rights spread throughout Europe in the wake of the French Revolution, European Jews were gradually invited to become citizens of the countries in which they lived, and as they adopted a new way of life, most Jews no longer looked to the rabbis as their authorities on religious matters. Most Jews still identified with Judaism, but they began to fashion new forms of Judaism to suit the new era that were at odds with the Judaism of the rabbis in prior centuries. Nonetheless, the Judaism of the rabbis remained central to these new forms of Judaism as well, even if the authority of the rabbis was much diminished.

The contribution of the rabbis to Judaism has been so distinctive that it is referred to by academics as "rabbinic Judaism," and I will use this label as well. However, the label is somewhat misleading. From the ninth to the nineteenth century, Jews would have been perplexed by the notion that there was such a thing as rabbinic Judaism. During these centuries, rabbinic Judaism was simply Judaism. A good way for Westerners to understand the role of rabbinic Judaism in the development of Judaism is to see it as serving a function similar to that which the New Testament served in Christianity. Just as the New Testament shaped the Hebrew Bible into the religion we know as Christianity, rabbinic Judaism shaped the Hebrew Bible into the religion we know as Judaism.

This section will explore rabbinic contributions to Judaism regarding the issue of violence. We will see that the rabbis largely adopted the theology of history in the Hebrew Bible but shaped it in light of their own circumstances and with the help of material extraneous to the Bible. What emerged was a biblical-rabbinic theology of history that had important implications for the manner in which Jews approached violence.

3.1 The Historical Background

We must first provide more information about rabbinic Judaism, and we will begin with the historical background that explains its emergence. As we saw in the previous section, the biblical history ends in the sixth century BCE at the beginning of the Second Temple period, a period in which Jews rebuilt their state while under Persian domination. The Persian period lasted for almost two centuries, but it came to an end in 332 BCE when Alexander the Great conquered the Jewish state en route to establishing his empire. A new period thus began for the Jews in which they were dominated by Greek rulers, and it too would last almost two centuries.

In 152 BCE, Jews were able to regain their independence for the first time in five centuries when the Maccabees overthrew Antiochus Epiphanes IV and the Seleucid dynasty that had inherited the portion of Alexander's empire encompassing the land of Israel. The Maccabees' victory resulted in the installation of the Hasmonean monarchs. This dynasty, however, was short-lived. In 63 BCE, Jews came under the domination of the Roman Empire, which was expanding rapidly at the time. Jews chafed under Roman rule, and they therefore rebelled in 66 CE with the hope of attaining independence once again. The rebellion took several years to put down, but finally, in 73 CE, the last pockets of resistance were extinguished at the fortress of Masada in the Judean desert. Most significantly, the Temple in Jerusalem was again destroyed. Jewish aspirations for achieving independence were not yet exhausted, and another Jewish rebellion against Roman rule broke out in 132. However, it too ended in defeat in 135.

It was at this at this time that the rabbis began to emerge as an identifiable group in the Jewish community, and they were faced with enormous challenges. Two failed rebellions against the Romans had decimated the Jewish community in the land of Israel and had left the country in ruins. Judaism's central shrine had once again been destroyed, and as the years went by, it became clear that it was not going to be rebuilt any time soon, as had happened after the destruction of the First Temple. Many Jews in this period must have been asking fundamental questions about their religious beliefs. Had the covenant with God been broken, and was this the reason for their suffering? And if the covenant was still in effect, what explained the catastrophes that Jews were experiencing? How would Jews continue worshipping God without the Temple that had been the center of their religion, the place in which the animal sacrifices had been performed? It was the rabbis who provided the most effective answers to these questions, and in doing so, they not only saved Judaism from demise; they gave it a renewed vitality that would allow it to thrive for centuries despite the hardships Jews would experience living under Christian and Muslim rule.

The rabbis were essentially religious sages who based their authority on their knowledge and skill in interpreting the Hebrew Bible. They not only were astute readers of the biblical text but also possessed a large body of oral traditions that supplemented the biblical text and filled in its gaps. According to the rabbis, these oral traditions constituted an entire second Torah that had been given to Moses on Mount Sinai alongside the written Torah, and these traditions had been passed down by word of mouth from generation to generation. The rabbis saw themselves as the guardians of this "Oral Torah," as they called it (Jaffee, 2006: 78–81, 161–62).

The rabbis used their expertise as biblical interpreters to convince the Jews that the covenant was still very much in place and that their suffering was due to their sins. The Jews had not kept their end of the covenantal bargain, and God was therefore punishing them (Goldenberg, 2006: 199). The rabbis also convinced the Jews that, if they repented of their sins and observed God's commandments, he would return them to their homeland and the Temple would again be rebuilt (Jaffee, 2006: 117–21; Schiffman, 2006). The rabbis based these predictions on passages in the Bible with which we are already familiar. We saw in the previous section that various passages in the biblical text predicted that, if the Jews were not obedient to God, they would be exiled from their land. However, God would eventually redeem them and restore the Davidic dynasty, the nations of the world would live in peace, and they would all recognize the God of Israel as the one true God. These forecasts seemed to have come true, in part, with the exile of the Jews to Babylonia in the sixth century BCE and their subsequent return to their homeland; however, the rest of the predictions remained unfulfilled. The rabbis therefore assumed that the prophetic predictions applied to their own situation. They believed that the exile foreseen in the Bible referred to the Roman destruction that had left the Jews in exile in the sense that they no longer had sovereignty in their homeland. They also believed that the predicted redemption lay in the future (Schiffman, 2006: 1054–56).

We should also add that the rabbis did not rely solely on the biblical text for their speculations here. They were also influenced by other texts written during the Second Temple period that never became part of the biblical canon. Some Jewish writers in this period were fascinated by the forecasts in the Bible about a future utopia, and they produced texts that greatly elaborated upon them. These texts also reshaped the predictions in some respects. For instance, a number of them couched the events leading up to the messianic era in apocalyptic terms. Just prior to this era, the world would be under the influence of evil cosmic forces represented by the nations oppressing Israel, but God would eventually wage war on those forces and come out victorious, thereby freeing Israel from its oppressors. Also, some of these texts depicted the messiah as more than just an heir to the Davidic dynasty; he was now portrayed as a supernatural being (Collins, 2010). The rabbis were apparently familiar with some of the ideas in these texts and absorbed them into their own thinking (Schiffman, 2006: 1056–60).

The major challenge for the rabbis was that, without the Temple, Jews were unable to perform animal sacrifices to worship God. How then could the Jews observe God's commandments and merit redemption? The rabbis confronted this problem with boldness and ingenuity. They believed that the written Torah and the Oral Torah were critical for guiding the Jews in observing the commandments in a post-Temple era. No, the Jews would not be able to perform sacrifices without the Temple in Jerusalem, but there were hundreds of other commandments the Jews could continue to observe to show God that they were still his chosen people and that they merited redemption (Goldenberg, 2006: 199–201). The rabbis also believed that the Oral Torah allowed them a certain amount of creativity so that they could institute new laws to replace those that had been lost. Thus, for instance, the rabbis ruled that, instead of performing sacrifices, the Jews could engage in communal prayer several times a day (Kimelman, 2006). Over a period of several hundred years, the rabbis developed their interpretations of the Torah's commandments into an entire system of laws that governed every aspect of Jewish life, again with the hope that, if Jews observed its imperatives, God would send his messiah and redeem them.

3.2 Violence

Let us now turn to our main concern, which is the issue of violence. We said in the previous section that the theology of history in the Hebrew Bible had within it the potential to inspire Jews to engage in violence. According to the Bible, God commanded the Israelites to wage war against nations that thwarted his covenantal plan – most notably, the Canaanites and the Amalekites – and we speculated that these wars might inspire later Jewish readers of the Bible to engage in violence against their enemies, even in the absence of an explicit divine directive. We also surmised that Jews might be especially inclined to do so, given that the messianic era predicted in the Bible would come about only after the nations that had oppressed the Israelites were punished for their sins. We can add here that the impetus for Jews to engage in violence for messianic purposes would have only been further strengthened by the apocalyptic texts that were produced in the Second Temple period. These texts drew attention to the messianic era, described the destruction of Israel's oppressors in that era in colorful detail, and assumed that its arrival was imminent.

The potential for Jews to engage in violence as a result of messianic expectations seems to have been realized in the two Jewish rebellions against Rome. There is evidence that one of the factors that inspired the first revolt in 66 CE was the belief that the messianic period was at hand and that Jews should therefore do their part to advance the messianic process. Josephus, a Jewish historian in this period whose writings provide invaluable information about the events leading up to the revolt, describes a number of other failed insurrections against the Romans that preceded this revolt and were inspired by messianic motivations (Horsley, 1992, 276–95; Schiffman, 2006: 1060).

We know less about the second rebellion against Rome in 132, but here too modern scholars speculate that messianic expectations played a role. This rebellion was led by Simeon bar Kosiba who seems to have been regarded by some Jews as the predicted messiah. He was renamed by his followers Simeon bar Kokhba, or "Simeon, son of the Star," which seems to have had messianic meaning. This name was based on a verse in the Torah, Numbers 24:17, which states that "a star shall come out of Jacob," and this verse was understood by some Jews at the time as a messianic prophecy. Most important, it would appear that some figures among the newly emergent rabbinic class were involved in the Bar Kokhba revolt and believed in its messianic significance. Rabbi Akiva, one of the most important and beloved rabbis of this period, appears to have supported the notion that Simeon bar Kokhba was the messiah (Marks, 1994; Schiffman, 2006: 1060–61).

However, the rabbis eventually chose a different path. As they reshaped Judaism over the next many centuries, the rabbis deliberately played down the messianic elements in the Hebrew Bible. They certainly believed that the messianic period would come, and they prayed for its arrival. However, the devastation caused by the two rebellions against Rome seems to have convinced the rabbis that the best way to bring about the messianic redemption was not through violent confrontation with their oppressors but by observing the biblical commandments as interpreted in rabbinic tradition; God would take care of the rest. This way of thinking was predicated on the belief that the real reason for the suffering of the Jews was their own failure to observe the commandments, not the actions of the Romans. The Romans were merely the means by which God was punishing the Jews for their failures. Thus, only by recommitting themselves to the observance of the divine commandments would the Jewish people be redeemed.

The rabbis continued to uphold this way of thinking in order to deal with the subjugation of Jews in other lands in subsequent centuries. The rabbis saw their situation in these lands as an extension of the punishment that God had brought upon the Jewish people for their sins in the Roman period, and the rabbis thus continued to preach to their followers that they needed to strictly obey the divine commandments if they were to be redeemed.

On the whole, the rabbis were not explicit about their opposition to the use of violence to initiate the process of redemption, but scholars cite numerous pieces of evidence suggesting that the rabbis did indeed take that position. For instance, in the liturgy that the rabbis composed for Jews to recite on a daily basis, prayers for messianic redemption generally assumed that it would come about because of the observance of the divine commandments and that the task of defeating oppressors of the Jewish people belonged to God and God alone (Berger, 2007: 54–55). The nonviolent thrust of this way of thinking comes through clearly in several rabbinic sources in which the rabbis describe a mythical scenario in which God forces the Jewish people to take an oath that, while they are in exile, they will not rebel against the gentile nations who rule over them, nor attempt to return en masse to the land of Israel. In these passages, the rabbis are clearly signaling to their followers that they should not engage in violent messianic activism (Babylonian Talmud, *Ketubot* 110b–111a; *Song of Songs Rabbah* 2:7).

Some rabbinic sources seem to reflect a desire to discourage violence as a means to bring about the messianic period by deemphasizing the messianic idea entirely. We find numerous statements in rabbinic literature that forbid Jews from speculating about when the messianic redemption will arrive, a practice that must have been common at the time (e.g., Babylonian Talmud, *Sanhedrin* 97b). Here again, it would seem that the rabbis were attempting to head off an inordinate focus on the messianic period, possibly because of the violence it might inspire.

The opposition of the rabbis to violent messianic activism seems to have morphed into a more general ethic of nonviolence. In several passages, the rabbis contrast the warring ways of Rome with the peaceful ways of Israel. Thus, we have the following dictum reported in the name of R. Hiyya: "[Moses] said to them [i.e., Israel]: 'If you see that he [i.e., Esau] seeks war against you, do not resist but hide from him until his world has passed'" (*Deuteronomy Rabbah* 1:19). The rabbis commonly identified Rome with Edom, the nation that descended from Esau, and thus, when Moses is described in this source as warning Israel not to respond to Esau's provocations, one can assume that the lesson concerns the Jews and their response to Roman aggression. Other rabbinic passages encouraged nonviolence with no reference to Rome. In one such passage, we are told that, "a man should always strive to be of the persecuted rather than of the persecutors because there is none among the birds more persecuted than doves and pigeons, and yet Scripture made them [alone among birds] eligible for the altar [i.e., sacrifice]" (Babylonian Talmud, *Bava Kamma* 93a). In another passage, the rabbis declare, "Who is the hero of heroes? One who transmutes foe into friend" (*Avot de-Rabi Natan*, version A, 23).

Often, the nonviolent ethic of the rabbis is couched in positive statements about the value of peace. For instance, the rabbis inform us that, "Great is peace for all blessings are contained in it . . . Great is peace for God's name is peace" (*Numbers Rabbah* 11:7). Many of the major prayers in the traditional Jewish liturgy composed by the rabbis conclude with a prayer for peace, including grace after meals, the *'amidah*, the priestly blessing, and the *kaddish*.

The nonviolent dimension of rabbinic Judaism is also evident in an important psychological shift that takes place among the rabbis regarding the issue of manhood. In their literature, the rabbis – who were all male – express pride in possessing virtues that in most cultures at the time would have been considered feminine, such as modesty, humility, meekness, and compassion. Conversely, virtues that would have been considered manly at the time, such as physical strength, violent behavior, and military prowess, were reinterpreted by the rabbis in nonviolent terms. The rabbinic statement just cited stating that a "hero" is one who "transmutes foe into friend" is a good example of this tendency. Heroism here is not military heroism; rather, it is the *avoidance* of military activity by reconciling with one's enemy. Another example of the same tendency is that the rabbis often depicted themselves as warriors – literally, as "the holders of the shields" (*ba'aley terisin*) – but not warriors in the conventional sense; they were warriors in the sense that they did battle with words in debating the meaning of God's Torah. Here, the rabbis have transmuted the violence of military activity into nonviolent argumentation (Boyarin, 1997: 1–186).

Some rabbis also attempted to soften the violence in the Bible. For example, there are several rabbinic passages that tell us that, before the Israelites entered the land of Canaan, God instructed Joshua to do his best to spare the Canaanite nations from annihilation by offering them the opportunity to depart from the land unharmed. Only one nation took Joshua up on this offer, according to the rabbis, and that nation was rewarded by God with another land (*Numbers Rabbah* 19:27; *Tanhuma Tsav* 3). No negotiation of this kind is recorded in the biblical text; the exchange depicted here is purely the product of the rabbinic imagination. Yet the purpose of this rereading of the biblical text is obvious. The rabbis were trying to show that the Canaanite genocide was not inevitable and that the Canaanites themselves could have avoided it had they only accepted God's offer to leave the land.

The rabbis also made efforts to soften the brutality of God's command to annihilate the Amalekites. For instance, an idea found in numerous rabbinic sources, particularly in the medieval period, is that the Amalekites represent the evil inclination in human beings. The implication here is that the command to annihilate the Amalekites is, in truth, an imperative to eradicate the propensity to sin within ourselves (Sagi, 1994: 330–36). It need not be understood as a call to physical violence against other human beings.

To sum up thus far, the rabbis seem to have taken Judaism in a direction very different from that of the Hebrew Bible with respect to the issue of violence. The Bible not only accepted violence as a legitimate means for the nation of Israel to achieve its aims; it often extolled such violence. However, the rabbis appear to have tacitly rejected this approach to violence. The thrust of their thinking was that Jews should not attempt to defeat their oppressors by waging war on them; such violence had only been self-destructive. Rather, Jews could achieve this goal by observing God's commandments and waiting patiently for God to reward them by taking care of their oppressors. If the Jews lived in accordance with God's will, he would send his messiah to free them from their overlords and redeem them.

This reading of the rabbis is the one most commonly accepted by modern Jewish scholars, and it is a reading with a long history. For the past century, Jewish academics, rabbis, and theologians have argued that the rabbis defanged the violence of the Hebrew Bible and put a nonviolent stamp on Judaism (Eisen, 2011: 69–70). However, as I have shown in a previous study, this reading of the rabbis is not entirely accurate. If we delve further into rabbinic literature, it becomes evident that the rabbis did not eschew violence to the extent that commentators have wanted to believe (Eisen, 2011: 97–109). Even if one accepts the notion that the rabbis opposed violence as a means to hasten the coming of the messianic era, this does not necessarily mean that the rabbis adopted a nonviolent ethic. Their reasons for rejecting violence as a way of bringing the messianic redemption may have been practical. They may have recognized that the Romans were simply too powerful to overthrow, and they therefore encouraged their followers to adopt another approach to achieve redemption: they should observe God's commandments with the hope that God himself would take violent action against Rome. If this was indeed what the rabbis were thinking, they did not renounce violence for messianic purposes. The notion that God would do the violent dirty work in the messianic redemption still contained the assumption that violence against the enemies of the Jewish people was at least part of the solution to their problems. Furthermore, the idea that God would take violent action against the nations oppressing the Jews still contained within it the danger that Jews would be inspired to participate in such violence, despite the wishes of the rabbis that they leave this matter to God (Eisen, 2011: 101–2).

As for violence in the Bible regarding past events, there are certainly indications that some rabbis were uncomfortable with the treatment of the Canaanites and the Amalekites, as we have seen. However, at no point did the rabbis renounce the violence against these nations. Their assumption was that such violence was entirely justified (Eisen, 2011: 104).

As for the Amalekites, the fact that the rabbis equated the Amalekites with the evil inclination did not mean that they rejected the literal meaning of the biblical text describing the war against them. In fact, it is inconceivable that the rabbis would have taken such a position; they accepted the events in the biblical text as accurate history. We therefore have to understand the identification of the Amalekites with the evil inclination as an interpretation that the rabbis *added* to the literal meaning of the biblical text, not as an interpretation that replaced that meaning.

Moreover, the rabbis had the tendency to identify the Amalekites with whichever nation or people was oppressing them at the time. Thus, for instance, in the Roman period, the rabbis identified the Amalekites with the Romans; in the medieval period, rabbis in Europe identified the Amalekites with Christendom. The Amalekites therefore became a versatile image that Jews could attach to any nation or people that was responsible for their suffering, and we must appreciate the serious implications of this way of thinking. By equating a nation with the Amalekites, the rabbis were saying, in effect, that the nation in question deserved to be annihilated (Cohen, 1991; Eisen, 2011: 104–5).

The picture that emerges here is that the rabbis never actually renounced the violence of the biblical past nor the violence of the messianic future. Nor did they necessarily renounce the use of violence in the present, at least not in principle. They may have merely recognized that the use of violence in the present was not possible without it being self-destructive and that Jews therefore had to pursue another path for dealing with their oppressors. At the very least, it is quite clear that the rabbis seethed with anger against their overlords. That is evident in their habit of identifying those who subjugated them with Amalekites. It is also evident in a myriad of sources in which they expressed deep resentment and hatred toward those who were responsible for Jewish suffering. Such anger could easily turn violent once again.

Thus, if the rabbis seemed to adopt a nonviolent ethic in some of their sources, there was another side to their thinking. Their nonviolence was certainly not of the thoroughgoing variety that we see in the principled pacifism of various groups throughout history, such as the Anabaptists in the Protestant Reformation or Mahatma Gandhi and his followers. For the rabbis, violence had a legitimate place in their thinking, even if they did their best to preempt Jews from using it in an unwise manner.

3.3 Conclusions

In conclusion, the rabbis adopted an ethic that was mostly nonviolent. Yet what scholars have not sufficiently recognized is that their worldview still contained within it elements that could result in the eruption of violence under the right circumstances.

The rabbis absorbed the theology of history in the Bible and applied it to their own circumstances. The predictions in the Bible regarding exile were about the destruction of the Jewish state at the hands of the Romans. Those concerning a future utopia were about the messianic era that was yet to come. The rabbis also adopted the biblical notion that the messianic era would be accompanied by violence, with God punishing the nations of the world that had oppressed the Jews.

One can imagine how Jews might come to the conclusion that, in light of this theology, they were obligated to help the redemption along by engaging in violence against their oppressors. In fact, this way of thinking had been taken up by some Jews in the two rebellions against Roman rule. The rabbis certainly discouraged such thinking for either moral or practical reasons, or both, and thus the judgment that they were nonviolent is accurate to some extent. Nonetheless, the rabbis did not renounce violence in principle; they continued to believe that the messianic period would be preceded by violence against those who subjugated them. This belief therefore kept open the possibility that the messianic idea would again inspire violence at some future point in time. All that was needed was for Jews to conclude, as some of them had in the two rebellions against Rome, that they could help the messianic era come to fruition by helping God defeat their enemies.

Social Identity Theory (SIT) is again very helpful in putting all of this into perspective. As we saw in the previous section, SIT teaches us that groups will often turn violent when they are under unusual stress, whether it be political, economic, or social. Well, by the time we get to the rabbinic period, Jews had been under nearly constant stress for roughly a millennium! From the eighth century BCE onward, they were subjugated in sequence by the Assyrians, Babylonians, Persians, Greeks, and Romans. The Hasmonean period between the Greeks and the Romans offered a respite, but it lasted less than a century. In light of this history and what SIT teaches us, it is no surprise that the rabbis harbored fantasies of revenge against their oppressors, fantasies that would sustain the possibility that Jews would engage in violence at some point in the future.

We can also invoke the work of Vamik Volkan, a psychiatrist whose insights shed valuable light on how the rabbis understood their situation. Volkan's work is focused on recent instances in which ethnic groups have been prone to violence. According to Volkan, one finds a common pattern in the thinking of these groups that explains their violent behavior. These groups have usually experienced a major trauma in their past that they repeatedly commemorate and that serves to consolidate their identity. The focus on this "chosen trauma," as Volkan calls it, renders them unable to move on from their past injuries and mourn what has been lost, and as a consequence, they are easily aroused to violence in order to redress these injuries (Volkan, 2007).

While Volkan applies these insights to recent events, they are clearly relevant for rabbinic Judaism. For the rabbis, the "chosen trauma" was the destruction of the Temple and the Jewish state by the Romans in the first century CE. By the medieval period, rabbinic Judaism had made this event central to Jewish identity and it was constantly commemorated in Jewish prayer and ritual. The rabbis set aside several days in the Jewish calendar as days of mourning and fasting for this purpose (Mishnah, *Ta'anit* 4:6). The only thing missing here was the ability of Jews to act on their chosen trauma in a violent manner, as Volkan's theory would predict, but that opportunity would not come until the modern period.

4 Medieval and Early Modern Judaism

In the medieval and early modern periods, Jews continued to live as a subjugated people as they had before the destruction of their state in the first century CE, but now most were living as exiles in foreign lands under Christian and Muslim rule. I would like to devote a brief but important section to a discussion of the difficulties that Jews faced in this lengthy span of time and how these difficulties affected their views of non-Jews. In some respects, Jewish life in exile became worse in the medieval and early modern periods, particularly under Christian rule, and this deepened the resentment that Jews felt toward their oppressors. As a result, Jews increasingly focused on the biblical-rabbinic theology of history that was central to their identity and longed for the messianic redemption that would bring an end to their travails. Jewish views of non-Jews also became even more negative, and this perspective was reflected in Kabbalah, which, by the end of the medieval period, had become the dominant theology in Judaism.

4.1 Jewish Life in the Medieval and Early Modern Periods

Let us begin by describing in general terms what life was like for Jews in the medieval and early modern periods, starting with medieval Europe.[4] Here

---

[4] The following historical survey summarizes events that are common knowledge among Jewish historians. Readers interested in an introductory treatment of these events should consult Efron et al. (2013), chapters 5–9.

the treatment of Jews was determined in large part by the Church. According to Church doctrine, Jews were to be tolerated because they had initially been God's chosen people, and even though they were no longer to be regarded as such, they continued to serve as witnesses to God's revealed truth in the Hebrew Bible. However, Jews were also to be kept in a lowly and humble condition because they had rejected Jesus and his message and were deemed responsible for his death.

In the early centuries of the medieval period, the Church's views had relatively little impact on European Jews. Europe was in a chaotic state as the Roman Empire disintegrated and the feudal system came into being. Because of this situation, the Church's reach was limited. In the later centuries of the medieval period, however, particularly after the eleventh, life in Europe started to settle down as states began to emerge, mechanisms were found to preserve public order, and Europe's economy began to grow. The Church took advantage of the newfound stability and became a more powerful institution with influence throughout Europe. Europeans also became more pious. As a result, the Church's attitudes toward Jews began to have an effect on how they were treated. Jews were now increasingly excluded from European life politically, socially, and economically.

Even worse, Jews were sometimes subject to outright violence. It was not uncommon for rulers to expel all Jews from their territories, often with little notice. In fact, between 1290 and 1570, Jews were banished from virtually every area of western and central Europe, with the exception of some regions in Germany and northern Italy. The expulsions were sometimes motivated by religious considerations; some rulers were loath to have a people in their lands that had rejected Christianity and were responsible for Jesus's death. Yet sometimes the expulsions were for economic reasons; in many places, Jews took up professions in which they competed with Christians, and thus rulers expelled Jews from their territories for the benefit of their Christian constituents.

We should pause to appreciate how traumatic these expulsions were. Jews were sent off on treacherous journeys by land or sea with whatever possessions they could carry, hoping to find another country that would take them in. Some Jews did. They were welcomed in Poland and the Ottoman Empire because they were seen as valuable for economic reason;

Jews had a reputation for being good businessmen. Many Jews, however, died before reaching safe haven.

Worst of all for medieval Jews was that thousands of them died in periodic anti-Jewish violence. Despite the Church's explicit instructions that the Jews be tolerated, mob violence sometimes broke out against them anyway. The first major instances of such violence took place during the First Crusade that began in 1096. Thousands of Jews lost their lives in central Europe to the Crusader armies as they marched across Europe on their way to the Holy Land.

The early modern period witnessed violence against Jews that was in some instances even worse. Most notably, in 1648, Ukrainian Cossacks rose up against the Polish regime that at that time ruled their territory and in the process massacred tens of thousands of Jews.

One does not want to exaggerate the hardships of Jews in medieval and early modern Europe. European Jews did quite well in some places and times. Still, life for the Jews in medieval and early modern Europe was precarious and insecure even in the best of times, and in the worst of times, intolerable.

Jews living in Muslim lands in the medieval and early modern periods fared much better than they did in Christian Europe. Muslims regarded Jews as monotheists and believed that they were recipients of genuine revelation from God in the form of the Torah. Therefore, in Islamic law, Jews were placed in the category of *dhimma*, which meant that they were a protected minority.

However, here too Jews experienced discrimination. Muslims believed that, while Jews had received genuine divine revelation, over time they had distorted its meaning. The same accusation was made against Christianity. According to Muslims, Islam was revealed to Muhammad to correct these distortions. Therefore, Judaism and Christianity were regarded by Muslims as inferior religions, and their adherents were subject to discriminatory laws that were meant to remind them of their errors. These laws were often not enforced, but the status of Jews and Christians in Muslim society was not equal to that of Muslims. Moreover, from time to time, violence erupted against Jews here as well. This violence was less frequent and less extreme than it was in Christian Europe but that did not make it any less traumatic for the Jews experiencing it.

4.2 Kabbalah

We saw in the previous section that the ill-treatment of Jews by non-Jews helped explain the anger that the rabbis expressed toward non-Jews in their literature. The same can be said about medieval and early modern rabbinic literature. In this literature as well, rabbis expressed anger toward non-Jews as a result of their continued subjugation. They continued to believe that their suffering was due to their sins, but they also believed that their Christian and Muslim overlords were sinners as well because of their bad treatment of Jews and that these oppressors would merit divine punishment when the messianic period began. These beliefs were not confined to rabbis; they were known by common Jews as well. The liturgy recited in synagogues repeatedly reminded Jews that their Temple had been destroyed and they had been exiled from their land due to their sins but that God would redeem them and punish their oppressors in the process.

However, a school of Judaism developed in the medieval period that expressed a hostility toward non-Jews that was more pronounced than that of rabbinic Judaism, and it is important that we understand its perspective. I am referring here to Kabbalah. Kabbalah is often understood as Jewish mysticism, but its impact on Judaism was not as much in promoting mystical experience as it was in contributing an entirely new theological system to Judaism. It began to emerge in France and Spain in the twelfth and thirteenth centuries and gradually developed over the next several centuries into a full-fledged theology. It also became increasingly popular; by the beginning of the seventeenth century, it had become the dominant theology in Judaism. Kabbalah was based on biblical and rabbinic Judaism, but it incorporated foreign ideas into its thinking, and what emerged from this mixture was a highly original approach to Judaism.

What is most important for our concerns is that the views of Kabbalah regarding non-Jews were highly negative. Kabbalah, in effect, accentuated the anger against non-Jews that had been expressed in rabbinic literature. A full explanation of these views would require a lengthy description of its complex theology, but for our purposes, we can encapsulate it in a few basic principles. According to Kabbalah, the entire non-Jewish world is nurtured by forces rooted in a metaphysical realm of evil. The souls of non-Jews are rooted in these forces and are therefore fundamentally different from the souls of Jews that are rooted in the realm of the divine. The Kabbalists also developed the belief that, when the messianic period arrived, the realm of evil would be destroyed and, along with it, the non-Jewish world that represented it on earth. Thus, what we have here is a dualistic system, in which the forces of good associated with the Jewish people are at war with the forces of evil associated with the non-Jewish world (Wolfson, 2006: 17–128).

The Kabbalists reserved special censure for the enemies of the Jews both past and present. The Canaanites and Amalekites were in that category, as were Christians and Muslims. According to the Kabbalists, these nations are particularly active in representing the forces of evil in the world and opposing the forces of goodness (Tishby, 1989: 68–71; Wolfson, 2006: 97–107, 129–85). Yet what is striking is that, for the Kabbalists, all non-Jews are enemies of the Jewish people by their very nature in embodying the forces of evil. Rabbinic literature had mixed views of non-Jews. Some rabbinic sources certainly expressed hostility toward non-Jews, but others had remarkably positive attitudes toward them (Eisen, 2011: 69–80). Thus, in identifying the non-Jewish world as uniformly evil, Kabbalah charted new territory in medieval Judaism. Moreover, the fact that Kabbalah became popularized meant that its negative views on non-Jews became widespread as well.

One should not be surprised by these ideas. They were the natural result of resentment Jews had accumulated for centuries regarding their subjugation to other nations. By the time the modern period began, Jews had been under the rule of foreigners for 2,400 years, with the exception of the Hasmonean period that lasted less than a century.

It is important to add here that not all Jewish thinkers in the medieval and early modern periods adopted a negative view of non-Jews of the kind found in Kabbalah. The main rival to Kabbalah in the medieval period was Jewish philosophy, which refers to schools that arose in the medieval period in which Jewish thinkers were devoted to constructing a theology based on rational argumentation. These schools openly borrowed insights from the great Greek philosophers of the ancient past, Plato and Aristotle, as well as Islamic philosophers who were similarly interested in Greek philosophy. The greatest representative of this approach to Judaism was Maimonides (1138–1204), perhaps the most significant figure in medieval Judaism. In contrast to Kabbalah, medieval Jewish philosophers, on the whole, saw no difference between Jews and non-Jews in principle when it came to their inherent nature. Moreover, the very fact that these thinkers relied on non-Jewish philosophy is itself a testimony to their more positive views of non-Jews by comparison with Kabbalah. The philosophers also did not see the messianic period as an era in which the non-Jewish world would be destroyed (Kellner, 1991). Yet, while Jewish philosophy competed with Kabbalah for several centuries, eventually Kabbalah became dominant and, with it, its strikingly more negative view of non-Jews.

4.3 Conclusions

In the medieval and early modern periods, the anger that Jews had developed against their oppressors in earlier periods was now transferred to their Christian and Muslim overlords. In some ways, though, that anger appears to have intensified as the centuries went by, Jews continued to be mistreated, and the messianic redemption was nowhere in sight. Kabbalah best reflected this tendency. The hatred that Jews felt toward their oppressors morphed into the idea that their suffering could be explained as the earthly manifestation of a cosmic war between the metaphysical forces of good and the metaphysical forces of evil. For now, the forces of evil manifested in the non-Jewish world had the upper hand, but, according to the Kabbalists, these forces would eventually be vanquished by the forces of good in the messianic era and with that victory would come messianic redemption. Here again, we can invoke Social Identity Theory (SIT). The kind of demonization of non-Jews found in Kabbalah is predicted by this theory. Any group that has been subjugated by another for an extended period of time is very likely to see its oppressors as inherently evil, even nonhuman.

These ideas certainly had within them the potential for spawning violence. If there was a war in the heavens between the forces of good and evil that was manifested on earth in the subjugation of Jews by their oppressors, it was not much of a leap for Jews to conclude that they should actively join the battle by going to war against their oppressors. However,

Jews in the medieval and early modern periods were in no better a position to act violently against their overlords than they had been in the early rabbinic period. Jews remained without any real political power, and they therefore had to be satisfied with the belief that their obedience to God would prompt him to defeat the enemies of his people on their behalf.

We should note here that the yearning for redemption did spawn a major messianic movement among Jews in the seventeenth century. The movement revolved around the figure of Shabbetai Tsevi, a Turkish Jew, whom many Jews believed to be the long-awaited messiah, and it was fueled in part by Kabbalah and its popular dissemination. The movement ended, for the most part, when Shabbetai was arrested by the Turkish authorities and was forced to convert to Islam. Yet what this episode demonstrates is the depth of Jewish yearning for messianic redemption. The Sabbatean movement, as scholars call it, was the most important messianic movement in Judaism since Christianity, and it engulfed a large portion of the Jewish world.

Jews would carry the emotions that fueled the Sabbatean movement into the modern period, which is the subject of the next section. However, this period would bring dramatic changes to the situation of Jews that would have an enormous impact on everything we have discussed thus far. These changes would deeply affect the way Jews viewed the biblical-rabbinic theology of history undergirding their identity and the longings for messianic redemption that this theology engendered. Most important, the potential for violence latent in these longings would be unleashed.

5 Modern Zionism

While there are disagreements about when the modern period begins for Jews, I will take the commonly held view that it was inaugurated by the French Revolution at the end of the eighteenth century when the Jews of France were granted citizenship and natural rights in a modern European state for the first time. However, for our purposes, the most important event in modernity would come a century and a half later with the establishment of the state of Israel. With the founding of a modern Jewish state in 1948, Jews regained political power and, along with it, the capability of engaging in violence on a mass scale. This section will therefore be devoted to understanding this development and its implications for the relationship between Judaism and violence.

5.1 The Historical Background

Let us begin with a summary of the historical background that led to the establishment of the state of Israel.[5] The emancipation of Jews in France was followed by their emancipation throughout the rest of Europe in the nineteenth century. The process was not a smooth one; it proceeded in fits and starts and experienced significant setbacks along the way. By 1880, though, most countries in Europe had granted citizenship and rights to their Jewish constituents similar to those granted in France. We should note that, by this time in history, European Jews constituted the majority of Jews in the world; in fact, by 1880, with the rapid growth of the Jewish population in eastern Europe, European Jews made up 88 percent of world Jewry (DellaPergola, 2001: 20). Therefore, the emancipation of Jews in Europe was, in effect, the emancipation of most Jews in the world at the time.

It goes without saying that, for Jews, the emancipation was momentous. They now had the same rights as everyone else in their respective countries, at least on paper, and Jews therefore looked forward to the prospect that the suffering they had experienced for centuries would be a thing of the past. However, the process of emancipation was also a time of great upheaval for European Jews. For centuries, they had lived their lives as outsiders in a European society that was often hostile to them, and they were now expected to participate in that society. Jews also had to grapple with unsettling questions about their Jewish identity in the new world they entered. Should they continue to live as Jews, and, if so, how? Should they retain their religious customs, and, if so, in what form?

Some European Jews decided to leave the Jewish community altogether. They converted to Christianity and joined the majority culture. Yet most Jews chose to remain as Jews, and the question for them was what shape

---

[5] As with my survey of historical events in Section 4, the following historical survey summarizes events that are common knowledge among Jewish historians. Readers interested in an introductory treatment of these events should consult Efron et al. (2013), chapters 10–13.

their Judaism would now assume. Some Jews believed that Judaism would not survive unless it was transformed and modernized. These Jews eventually coalesced into a denomination known as Reform Judaism, and it became extremely popular in western and central Europe. Some Jews preferred to remain separate from European society as much as possible and live according to the same laws and customs that had been at the center of Jewish life for centuries. These Jews eventually became known as Orthodox Jews, and they made up the vast majority of Jews in eastern Europe where the emancipation of Jews had proceeded at a much slower pace than in the rest of Europe. A third denomination eventually sprang up that endorsed changes to Judaism in light of modernity but was unwilling to go as far as the Reform movement did. This denomination eventually became known by the misleading name, Conservative Judaism. They were, in fact, "conservative," but only in relation to the Reform movement, not in relation to Orthodox Judaism.

Most important for our concerns is that Reform Jews were inclined to rethink the biblical-rabbinic theology of history that had anchored Jewish identity for centuries. Because they were enthusiastic about joining European society and saw a bright future ahead of them in being part of it, they saw no need to continue to believe in messianic redemption, at least not in any literal sense. In fact, upholding such a belief was a liability because it signaled to their non-Jewish neighbors that they were not fully loyal to the states in which they were now citizens. Some Reform congregations therefore dropped references to the messianic redemption from their liturgy to make clear to their fellow non-Jewish countrymen that they were loyal citizens of the states in which they lived (Meyer, 1988: 49, 122). Thus, the potential for violence inherent in Jewish messianism was now completely neutralized. Instead of praying for a return to their homeland, Reform Jews now spoke of an everlasting brotherhood between Jews and Christians that would draw from the best of the two religious traditions in order to build a better world. In fact, some Reform Jewish thinkers saw this outlook as the new messianism. Messianism was now conceived in terms of an everlasting peace in this world and was denuded of its nationalistic and violent elements (Beiser, 2018: 163–66, 291–94).

These views were anathema to Orthodox Jews. Jews in this denomination continued to uphold the biblical-rabbinic theology of history that was sketched out in previous sections and for centuries undergirded Jewish identity. Of course, this meant that Orthodox Jews still retained views of messianic redemption that carried the potential for violence, but they were not in a position to act on it any more than Jews had been before the modern period began. They were still a powerless minority.

Yet more momentous changes were in store for Jews in Europe. In the year 1881, anti-Jewish violence returned. The violence erupted suddenly in eastern Europe, and over the next two years, mobs attacked 200 Jewish communities in this part of Europe, leaving 40 Jews dead and thousands wounded and homeless. The Russian government, which ruled this area at the time, not only failed to intervene but encouraged the violence by suggesting that the Jews were the source of Russia's problems. Attacks on Jewish communities, now called "pogroms," continued over the next several decades. In 1903, a pogrom broke out against the Jewish community in Kishinev, a city that today is in Moldova. In 1905, Kishinev was attacked again along with Jewish communities in 300 other cities in the same part of Europe. In 1919–21, Jewish communities in Ukraine were victim to the worst violence Jews had experienced in the modern period. Here, pogroms claimed the lives of some 60,000 Jews over two years.

The Jews of western and central Europe did not experience violence of this kind, but they did witness the revival of virulent antisemitism, which became popular in these parts of Europe in the second half of the nineteenth century. The Dreyfuss affair became emblematic of this antisemitism. In 1894, Alfred Dreyfuss, the only Jew on the General Staff of the French army, was convicted of treason. The evidence leading to Dreyfuss's conviction turned out to be forged, and he was fully exonerated in 1906, but in the meantime, French antisemitism had emerged in full force. Dreyfuss certainly had his defenders among the French public. Yet a significant sector of French society not only believed the charges against Dreyfuss but was quite vocal about its belief that Dreyfuss was acting on behalf of a vast Jewish conspiracy bent on undermining France and its military. The hatred of Jews ignited by this group persisted in right-wing political circles in France even after Dreyfuss was proven innocent.

As all these events unfolded in Europe and Russia at the end of the nineteenth century and the beginning of the twentieth, Jews were shocked – even those who were not direct victims of the hatred and violence. After almost a century of watching the process of their emancipation unfold, Jews had come to believe that the hatred against them of earlier centuries was on its way out, as was the violence that accompanied it. It was now clear that this was not the case.

Reactions among Jews to these developments varied. Most Jews in western and central Europe continued to hold out hope that the emancipation process would get back on track. The Jews of eastern Europe and Russia, where actual violence against Jews had erupted, were less confident about this prospect, and millions of them fled to the United States with the hope that life for Jews would be different there.

Yet a small group of European Jews began to propose a new and radical idea: Jews needed to have their own state. Jews would never be safe in Europe or elsewhere living under non-Jewish rule; history had proven so. This group of Jews also came to believe that the best place for a Jewish state was Palestine, the location of the ancient Jewish homeland. As the group of Jews who supported this aspiration began organizing themselves into a movement, the term "Zionism" was coined. It was based on the biblical word, "Zion," which has several meanings but in some contexts in the biblical texts refers to the land of Israel.

The Zionists understood the steep odds against them. Palestine was ruled by the Turkish Ottoman Empire, and while it was in a relatively undeveloped corner of the empire, the Turks would not just give it away to the Jews. Moreover, to succeed at such a venture, Jews would need immense resources, political and financial. Yet the Zionists proceeded with their plans anyway, feeling that they had no other choice. In 1881, just after the first of the pogroms in Russia erupted, Jews who supported the notion of a modern Jewish state in Palestine began emigrating there in order to build settlements.

However, it was Theodor Herzl (1860–1904), a Hungarian Jew, who was mainly responsible for galvanizing Zionism into an international movement. He was residing in Vienna and working as a playwright and journalist when the Dreyfuss affair erupted, and he was shocked by the depth of the antisemitism that this event brought forth. Herzl began to identify with Zionism and soon became its leading figure. In 1897, he organized the first Zionist Congress in Basel, Switzerland, for the purpose of coordinating the efforts of Jews throughout Europe who supported Zionism. These efforts included raising funds to buy land in Palestine and establishing Jewish settlements there, as well as lobbying various governments in Europe to support the Zionist vision.

Herzl died young and just when these efforts were getting underway, but capable figures in the Zionist movement were able to carry on his work. After the First World War, Palestine fell under British control, which at first was a boon to the Zionist movement. The British were favorable to Zionism and even issued the Balfour Declaration in 1917, which declared their support for a national Jewish homeland in Palestine. However, the British turned out to be unreliable allies primarily because of the deteriorating relationship between Jews and Arabs in Palestine. Arab opposition to Zionism forced the British to rethink their relationship to the movement.

Under these circumstances, it was inevitable that violence would erupt between Jews and Arabs in Palestine. Palestinians had no interest in living in a Jewish state and saw it as an affront that Jews were planning to build such a state on land that they regarded as their own. Violence between the two groups first came in the form of small clashes, and as more Jews arrived in Palestine and purchased more land to settle, the scale and scope of the violence increased. It came to a head in 1936 with a full-scale rebellion by Palestinians against British rule and the Jewish presence in Palestine. The rebellion lasted three years, and in response to it, Britain attempted to appease the Palestinians by severely limiting Jewish immigration to the region.

When the Palestinian rebellion petered out in 1939, Europe was on the eve of the Second World War, an event that would have a big impact on the situation in Palestine. By the time the war concluded in 1945, the Holocaust had claimed the lives of 6 million Jews, fully one-third of the Jewish population of the world at the time. Jews had experienced numerous catastrophes in their history, but none quite like this.

With Jewish life in Europe having been mostly obliterated, Jewish refugees now flooded into Palestine, making tensions with the Palestinians even worse. The situation there was becoming increasingly unmanageable, and Britain finally decided to withdraw from Palestine and recommend that the land be partitioned into two states – one Jewish and one Arab. The newly formed United Nations voted on the partition plan in 1947 and approved it. The Jewish state formally declared independence in 1948 and became the state of Israel.

For most Jews, this event was of enormous significance. They now had an independent state in their ancient homeland for the first time in more than two thousand years. Palestinians and the Arab nations, however, were outraged and immediately waged war on the Jewish state. Israel won that war and even enlarged itself, but in the process, hundreds of thousands of Palestinians lost their homes and became refugees. In subsequent decades, the conflict continued. War between Israel and one or more of the surrounding Arab nations broke out in 1956, 1967, 1973, 1982, and 2006.

The Six-Day War in 1967 was particularly significant. Israel won this war resoundingly and greatly increased its size, capturing the Sinai Peninsula, the Gaza Strip, the Golan Heights, the West Bank, and East Jerusalem. Shortly after its victory, Israel began to establish Jewish settlements on the conquered land. The impetus for this initiative came primarily from a religious sector of Israeli society that believed that the establishment of Israel was the beginning of the messianic redemption, that the land captured in the Six-Day War would be part of the future messianic state, and that the land therefore had to be settled by Jews lest the Israeli government give it back as part of a peace agreement. Palestinians in the West Bank and Gaza, however, were enraged by the settlements and their subjugation under Israeli rule. Eventually, they initiated two major rebellions against Israeli rule, in 1987–93 and 2000–5. Israel relinquished control of Gaza to its Palestinian inhabitants in 2005, and it was soon taken over by Hamas, a militant group sworn to the destruction of Israel. Since then, Israel and Hamas have engaged in several wars.

At the time of this writing, Israel's relationship with its Arab neighbors has greatly improved. It has signed peace treaties with Egypt (1979), Jordan (1994), and the United Arab Emirates (2020). It is also developing ties with other Arab states. However, Israel's relationship with the Palestinians is as troubled as ever. Israel maintains control over the West Bank, home to millions of Palestinians who despise living under Israeli rule. Gaza remains under Hamas and maintains its hostility to Israel. A peace deal that would allow for the establishment of a Palestinian state in the West Bank and Gaza and put an end to Israel's conflict with the Palestinians has been elusive, and the number of Palestinians living in refugee camps in surrounding Arab countries has grown into the millions. Israel's greatest enemy, however, is not any of the Arab states, nor the Palestinians, but Iran. Iran has declared its desire to destroy Israel and has troops or affiliated militias entrenched in Lebanon and Syria, countries that border Israel.

As I said in my introductory section, I will not engage in a discussion of who is right or wrong in the Middle East conflict because that question is not relevant to my main concern, which is the relationship between Judaism and violence. Moreover, this question is one that is not easily answered. It will be sufficient to acknowledge that there are two narratives here representing the two sides of the conflict, both of which read the history of the Middle East conflict selectively and with a heavy hand of interpretation.

The Israeli narrative is that the establishment of the state of Israel represents a return by Jews to their rightful homeland that they lost in the first century CE and to which they never gave up their claim. Moreover, returning to their homeland was necessary. There was no place where Jews could live without being oppressed and persecuted because non-Jews had an irrational hatred of Jews that was incurable. However, Israel was not created with the intention of engaging in violence against Palestinians. The first Jewish settlements were established on land that was purchased from its Arab owners. In general, the Jewish attitude toward the Palestinians was one of good will; they hoped to be able to improve the lives of Palestinians, most of whom were poor farmers, by including them in a modern state. If there was hostility between Jews and Palestinians, it was initiated by the Palestinians who were negatively disposed to Jews as most non-Jews were. Therefore, when engaging in violence, Jews were merely defending themselves (Adwan, Bar-On, & Naveh, 2012).

The Palestinian narrative is that the land did not belong to the Jews but to them. They had inhabited it for generations and were its inhabitants when the Zionists arrived to establish settlements. From the very beginning of Zionism, its adherents intended to dispossess the Palestinians of their land. For this purpose, Zionism got assistance from the West that saw the establishment of a Jewish state in Palestine as an opportunity to consolidate Western influence in the Middle East. Zionism was thus an extension of Western colonialism that had a long history in the region. Therefore, Palestinians engaged in violence against Zionist settlers to defend themselves and their land (Adwan, Bar-On, & Naveh, 2012).

This summary does not do justice to the complexities of the two narratives. It also does not account for the many variations on each narrative. Yet the summary here is useful in providing an idea of the basic positions held by both sides of the Middle East conflict and why they have so far been unbridgeable.

5.2 Violence in Secular Zionism

The major question is what role religion has played on the Jewish side of the Middle East conflict. To what extent did Judaism encourage Jews to engage in violence – be it defensive or aggressive – in order to establish their own state and maintain it?

There is good reason to doubt that religion has had anything to do with the violence that Jews have engaged in for the sake of Zionism, at least up to the Six-Day War in 1967. When Zionism came into existence at the end of the nineteenth century, it was largely a secular phenomenon. It was a movement consisting of Jews who mostly rejected religion. In fact, many of the early Zionists were atheists. The basis of Zionism was the belief that the biblical-rabbinic theology of history that had been at the core of Jewish identity for centuries was no longer tenable. Jews had observed God's commandments and had waited patiently for him to reward them by bringing about the messianic redemption, but that way of life had brought nothing but misery. Jews could only watch passively as their non-Jewish oppressors persecuted them and humiliated them. The Zionists therefore argued that it was time for Jews to give up on religion as a means for their salvation and take matters into their own hands. Jews would experience relief from their suffering only by returning to their homeland and rebuilding their state on their own initiative. The early Zionists also envisioned the future Jewish state as secular. The identity of its citizens would be based on nationalism, not religion. What would bind them together would be factors that bind most nations together, such as a common history, language, and literature, and religion was not needed for this purpose. When the state of Israel was finally founded in 1948, this secular vision was realized. The first Israeli government was formed by the largest political faction of Zionism, Labor Zionism, which was secular and socialist in orientation, and it would remain in power for the first thirty years of the state. Israel's population has also been largely secular throughout its history. The precise percentage of the population that belongs in this category depends on how one defines secularity, but up to 80 percent of Israel's Jewish citizens are secular or have secular tendencies (Pew Research Center, 2016).

The secular vision of Zionism was possible, in part, because Judaism had never been just a religion. Judaism was also a marker of ethnic identity. Traditional Judaism had always recognized that what made someone Jewish had nothing to do with religious belief or practice; instead, it was based on genealogy. According to Jewish law, a Jew was defined as someone whose mother was Jewish. If that individual did not accept the beliefs or practices of Judaism, the rabbis regarded them as a bad Jew – but they were a Jew nonetheless. For this reason, when Jews were emancipated in European countries in the nineteenth century, many of them rejected Judaism as a religion but still considered themselves to be Jews from an ethnic standpoint. They saw themselves as bound to other Jews by history and Jewish moral values even as they denuded these facets of their identity of religious meaning. As a result, these Jews continued to socialize primarily with other Jews and to marry other Jews. Thus, well before there was a modern Jewish state, it was possible to be a Jew without religion. For the early Zionists, Zionism was merely a new way to be Jewish in this manner (Mandel, 2009; Biale, 2011).

In light of these observations, it does not seem possible that the violence Jews have engaged in to create and maintain the state of Israel has been due to religion. Yet an argument can be made that religion has still played a role here. A number of scholars have maintained that mainstream secular Zionism did not turn its back on religion entirely; rather, it unconsciously absorbed some of its most basic ideas and secularized them, and this perspective has important ramifications for the issue of violence.

Some scholars have claimed that secular Zionism was in large part a secularized form of traditional Jewish messianism. After all, the goal of secular Zionism was to redeem the Jewish people from the hardships of exile by bringing them back to their ancient homeland, an idea that was at the core of traditional Jewish messianism. Moreover, the inspiration for this secular messianism came, in part, from Judaism's most sacred text: the Hebrew Bible. Secular Zionists looked to the Bible as the basis of the Jewish claim to the land of Israel. In addition, secular Zionists spoke of themselves as being driven by an all-consuming faith in their mission, a faith that the Zionist enterprise would succeed despite all the odds heaped against it, and this faith had a great deal in common with the faith that traditional Jews had in their special relationship with God. Of course, secular Zionism denuded these ideas of Judaism of their supernatural meaning. The redemption of the Jewish people would come solely through human initiative. The land of Israel was no longer the "Holy Land" but was now a mundane national homeland. The faith that secular Zionists had in their mission in no way involved a personal God. Still, a good case can be made that these ideas had religious roots (Luz, 2003: 66–90, 103–14; Eisen, 2011: 167–75).

Highly instructive here is the manner in which secular Zionists used the victory of the Hasmoneans in the second century BCE against their Greek-Syrian overlords as inspiration for their own actions. In rabbinic tradition, the rabbis had focused on the miraculous nature of this victory on the belief that it was brought about through divine will (Babylonian Talmud, *Shabbat* 21b). The secular Zionists happily co-opted the Hasmonean victory by playing down the role of the divine and focusing on the faith that the Hasmoneans had in their own military prowess despite the long odds against their success (Shapira, 1992: 104; Luz, 2003: 106). In this way, secular Zionists made the Hasmoneans into role models for their own efforts.

If these observations are correct, they shed valuable light on the willingness of mainstream secular Zionists to use violence to accomplish their goals. The adaptation of messianism to the goals of secular Zionism is particularly important. As we have seen, the messianic concept represented the longing that Jews had for returning to their homeland so that they could live as a free and independent people, but it also represented the redressing of centuries of mistreatment by the non-Jewish nations through God's violent vengeance against them. Thus, if secular Zionists were indeed inspired by Jewish messianism, they were co-opting an element of Judaism that had long been associated with violence against non-Jews, and this would help explain the willingness of secular Zionists to take up arms for their cause.

Our case here is strengthened by the insights of scholars regarding modern Western nationalism. Scholars have long argued that, in the modern West, nationalism in its various manifestations was, in many respects, a sublimation of religion. As the West became more secular in the modern period, Westerners were inclined to replace religion as a focal point for social identity with nationalism. Moreover, the violence that often accompanied religion was transferred to nationalism as well. Wars that were once fought over religious differences were now fought over competing nationalisms. The same processes may have occurred in secular Zionism. It too may have replaced religion with nationalism while transferring the violent potential of the former to the latter as well (Eisen, 2011: 171–72).

Caution is in order here. We are dealing with subconscious processes about which we have little hard evidence. Furthermore, secular Zionism and Jewish messianism may have been separate outgrowths of common features of human psychology. It is normal for people to long for a national home and a better world, desires that both secular Zionism and Jewish messianism encompassed, and if that is the case, the connection between secular Zionism and Jewish messianism may not have been a direct one. Nonetheless, it is at least plausible that mainstream secular Zionists unwittingly absorbed elements of Jewish messianism, including its violent aspects.

There were certainly other factors responsible for this violence. Most secular Zionists explained their need to resort to violence in terms of simple self-defense. As noted in Section 5.1, the common Jewish narrative regarding the Middle East conflict has been that the violence between Jews and Arabs began with the Arabs and that Jews had no choice but to use violence in turn to protect themselves. In fact, early secular Zionists encapsulated this way of thinking in a Hebrew slogan – "*ein bereirah*," which means "there is no choice" – that is, Jews had no alternative but to use violence (Luz, 2003: 87–88, 204–8; Eisen, 2011: 196).

Yet this way of thinking can also be traced to Jewish sources. In Judaism, the right to engage in violence for the purpose of self-defense is a sacrosanct principle. The Talmud teaches that, "he who come to slay you, slay him first" (Babylonian Talmud, *Sanhedrin* 72a). Of course, secular Zionists did not need to cite a Jewish source to justify their actions. The principle of self-defense has been widely accepted by human beings in different cultures throughout history. Still, it can be argued that here, as well, secular Zionists based their thinking on an ethic ingrained in Jews over many centuries.

Our observations thus far about violence in secular Zionism have been about mainstream secular Zionism, which was left-wing in orientation, but similar observations apply to secular Zionism on the right. Supporters of this form of Zionism were in the minority in the early years of the movement and in the first decades after Israel came into existence, but in the past forty years, they have been highly influential in Israeli politics.

The largest right-wing faction of early Zionism was the Revisionist party, and its founder and chief ideologue was Vladimir Ze'ev Jabotinsky (1880–1940). Jabotinsky believed that the conflict between the Jews and the Palestinians would be settled only by military means. He and his followers were therefore more militant than the majority of Zionists who affiliated with the left and tended to view violence in more defensive terms. Jabotinsky's party also spun off smaller factions that were more extreme than his. The best known were Etsel (an acronym for the National Military Organization) – often referred to as "the Irgun," which was Hebrew for "organization" – and Lehi (an acronym for Fighters for the Freedom of Israel) – which was known as "the Stern Gang" on account of the surname of its founder. These groups were paramilitary organizations that targeted British government officials and military personnel in Palestine when the British pulled back from supporting the Jewish side in Palestine. Once the state of Israel was created, right-wing secular Zionism continued as a force in Israeli politics and society. In 1973, Menachem Begin, a former leader of the Irgun, formed the right-wing Likud political party. It came to power in 1977 and has been a major player in Israeli politics ever since.

The argument can be made that right-wing secular Zionists drew inspiration from Judaism in the same way that left-wing Zionists did in that they too unwittingly absorbed messianic motifs from Judaism and their violent potential. Yet the most militant representative of right-wing secular Zionism prior to 1948 relied on a number of other religious sources for their views, and here we are not speculating about subconscious processes; these Zionists used religious sources explicitly, and they therefore provide the clearest example of how religion was used by secular Zionism for violent purposes.

These Zionists cited the Bible as inspiration for their violent views more than other early secular Zionists did. More important for them than messianism were the wars the Israelites waged against their enemies. These were seen as paradigmatic of the kind of militarism that Jews should adopt in their quest to establish a Jewish state. Thus, the conquest of the Canaanites and the war against the Amalekites were prototypical of the kind of aggressive violence Jews should emulate. However, these Zionists also found inspiration in the other wars the Israelites waged. They contended that the role models for modern Jews should no longer be the pious rabbis who study all day, but biblical figures, such as King David who was a highly skilled military leader and was capable of brutality in his dealings with his enemies (Luz, 2003: 54–55; Eisen, 2011: 173–74).

These Zionists found particular inspiration in the two Jewish revolts against Rome in the first and second centuries CE. For them, the messianic element in these rebellions was far less interesting than the simple willingness of Jews to use violence to secure their freedom from foreign rule. These Zionists were also inspired by the mass suicide committed by the last holdouts in the Bar Kokhba revolt at Masada in 73 CE. These Jews were willing to take their own lives rather than be enslaved to the Romans. The same Zionists vilified the rabbis for having surrendered to Rome (Luz, 2003: 55–60).

5.3 Religious Zionism

Among the factions in Zionism, the connection between Judaism and violence is perhaps strongest in religious Zionism. This faction of Zionism consists of Orthodox Jews, and it has always been small relative to other Zionist factions. Since the Six-Day War in 1967, however, its influence on Israeli politics and society has been well out of proportion to its numbers due to the project it has overseen of building Jewish settlements in the territories captured by Israel in the Six-Day War, particularly the West Bank. This project has been controversial both in Israel and in the international community because Palestinians want this land for their own independent state as part of an overall peace agreement with Israel, and therefore the settlement project is regarded by them and many outside observers as a major obstacle to such an agreement. Nonetheless, religious Zionists have steadily placed Jewish settlers on this land, and currently, the settlements in the West Bank are home to half a million Israelis (Shimoni, 1995: 127–65).

Religious Zionism appeared early on in the Zionist movement. When Zionism started to become active at the end of the nineteenth century, Orthodox Jews were not inclined to join the new movement because of its staunch secularism. However, a small number did, and there were soon enough Orthodox Jewish Zionists to form a small but distinct faction within Zionism. These Zionists also began to produce leaders who had a variety of views on the meaning of the Zionist enterprise (Shimoni, 1995: 129–36). One of the most prominent of these individuals, and the one most important for our concerns, was R. Abraham Isaac Kook (1865–1935). R. Kook was born in eastern Europe and emigrated to Palestine in his adult years to support the Zionist enterprise; he soon became an important figure in its burgeoning Jewish community. In 1921, R. Kook was appointed Chief Rabbi of the Ashkenazi community in Palestine, and he served in that post until his death in 1935 (Shimoni, 1995: 145).

R. Kook did not live to see the creation of the state of Israel, but he developed a bold and dramatic theology of Zionism that eventually became highly influential in religious Zionist circles. According to this theology, Zionism was the beginning of the long-awaited messianic redemption. Other religious Zionists did not see Zionism in these terms. They were interested in creating a Jewish state for the same reasons that most secular Zionists were; it would provide a place of refuge for Jews. Many religious Zionists also spoke about the spiritual advantages of establishing a Jewish state. It would allow religious Jews to live their way of life more freely than in the diaspora, and they would do so in the land that had a special holiness to it. However, R. Kook took the religious significance of Zionism to a new level by understanding it in light of messianic redemption (Shimoni, 1995: 145–51).

To understand R. Kook's position, one has to be aware that messianism in Judaism comes in two forms. The more common one can be called "passive" messianism. According to this type of messianism, the messianic period will come about through God's sudden and direct intervention in history. The messianic redemption will therefore be miraculous in nature, as will the period inaugurated by it. This type of messianism is "passive" in that it is predicated on the belief that God will guide the events of the messianic process, not human beings. However, some Jewish sources speak of another form of messianism that can be called "active messianism," in which the role of human beings is central. According to this form of messianism, the messianic era will unfold in a less dramatic manner. It will evolve gradually in the course of ordinary human events, divine miracles will not be necessary, and its progress will therefore be guided, in part, by human will. For this reason, it may be difficult to discern whether the messianic period has even arrived. One will know that this is the case only when the messianic era is in its advanced stages (Myers, 1991).

R. Kook believed that Zionism was the beginning of messianic redemption because he supported the notion of active messianism. The formation of the Zionist movement and the establishment of Jewish settlements in Palestine were proof to him that the messianic process was underway. The return of Jews from their exile, long ago predicted in the Bible as the central event of the messianic period, was taking place. Orthodox Jews therefore had to support Zionism. The fact that Zionism was mainly a secular phenomenon was the biggest challenge to R. Kook's thinking, but it did not deter him. He came to believe that the secular Zionists were being inspired by the divine spirit to move the messianic process forward, even though they were not aware of it; and as the process continued, they would eventually realize that their actions were being guided by God and would return to religion (Shimoni, 1995: 147–48).

With respect to the issue of violence, most religious Zionists in the early years of Zionism took an approach that was similar to that of mainstream secular Zionism; violence was permitted only for the purpose of self-defense. However, in this period, religious Zionists were more committed to exercising restraint regarding the use of the violence than secular Zionists were. For instance, R. Isaac Jacob Reines (1839–1915), one of the leading religious Zionists, spoke about the need for religious Zionists to uphold the culture of "the Book" against the culture of "the Sword" upheld by the non-Jewish world. Thus, when Palestinians engaged in violence against Jews prior to the establishment of the state of Israel, the leading religious Zionists rabbis in Palestine were often at the forefront of attempts to rein in secular Zionists who called for revenge (Holzer, 2009: 167–77; Eisen, 2011, 187).

R. Kook's views on violence were unusually negative. He believed that violence had no place in the creation of a Jewish state. Zionism was the harbinger of the messianic period in which peace would reign throughout the world, and therefore the Zionist enterprise had to provide a model for peaceful behavior. R. Kook's views here were shaped in part by the First World War. Some sources in the rabbinic tradition espoused the view that the messianic period would be preceded by war between the nations of the world. The world would descend into chaos before the everlasting peace of the messianic era would take hold. R. Kook therefore believed that the First World War was another sign that the messianic period was indeed at hand. Here was the strife that had been predicted to precede the messianic redemption. Zionism, however, in R. Kook's thinking, would serve as the antidote to this strife. As the vehicle for the messianic redemption, it would provide a model of peace for the world to follow in anticipation of the messianic era (Holzer, 2009: 98–105).

R. Kook did not leave a large group of followers, but he did leave a sizeable body of writings that expressed his views in remarkably eloquent and passionate terms, and his son, R. Tsevi Yehudah Kook, gathered around him a small cadre of disciples who were devoted to preserving and propagating his father's teachings. However, R. Tsevi Yehudah also radicalized these teachings. He came to believe that violence had a legitimate place in Zionism and its messianic mission. After the state of Israel was created, R. Tsevi Yehudah spoke of Israel's army and its wars as being "holy" because they were critical for advancing the messianic process. He thus injected a militancy into this father's views that was at odds with their original intent (Luz, 2003: 223–24; Holzer, 2009: 203–48).

Most significant for R. Tsevi Yehudah Kook was a source from Moses Nahmanides (1194–1270), a rabbi of great stature in the medieval period. Nahmanides took the unusual position that, in the biblical narrative, God's commandment to Joshua and the Israelites to conquer the land of Israel and settle it was not a one-time imperative; it was eternally in force. Thus, the original conquest of the land did not fulfill this commandment once and for all. Jews were required to conquer and settle the land in any subsequent period in which the land was ruled by non-Jews (Holzer, 2009: 226–28). For R. Tsevi Yehudah, Zionism provided the opportunity for fulfilling this imperative.

The reasons for R. Tsevi Yehudah radically reshaping his father's teaching are not difficult to find. He had to make sense of traumatic events that his father did not live to see and that challenged his father's messianic theology. The most important of these was the Holocaust. Of course, R. Tsevi Yehudah also witnessed the creation of the state of Israel that, for him, represented a huge step forward in the messianic process, but this triumph was immediately followed by the 1948 war in which the Arab side did its best to destroy the nascent Jewish state and in which thousands of Jews were killed. These events seem to have convinced R. Tsevi Yehudah that the teachings of his father had to be reinterpreted in a militant vein. Yet, whatever the reasons for this reinterpretation, the approach of R. Tsevi Yehudah to Zionism represented an important shift in religious Zionism toward a worldview that was far more comfortable with the use of violence than earlier religious Zionists had been.

R. Tsevi Yehudah and his supporters had little influence on Israel's affairs until the Six-Day War in 1967. For R. Tsevi Yehudah, Israel's remarkable victory was the clearest evidence yet that the messianic era was unfolding. The territory captured in this war included a large portion of the land that God had promised to Abraham in the Bible, and, according to Jewish tradition, the borders of this land would be the same as those of the Jewish state in messianic times. If Israel's victory was not a sign that the messianic process was moving forward, what was? R. Tsevi Yehudah did not preach that Israel should wage unprovoked war against the surrounding Arab countries in order to enlarge Israel so that it would encompass the land designated for the messianic kingdom. However, he seems to have felt that, if the Arab countries waged war against Israel, it was a divinely ordained opportunity to conquer territory that was predicted to be part of the messianic kingdom, and the Six-Day War had clearly been an opportunity of this kind (Sprinzak, 1991: 43–46).

However, in the wake of the Six-Day War, there was much talk in Israeli society that Israel should trade the conquered land for peace with its Arab neighbors, and therefore R. Tsevi Yehudah began to mobilize his followers to ensure that this would not happen. They started to lobby the Israeli government not only to retain the conquered land but to establish Jewish settlements on it so that it would never be relinquished. The government was initially hesitant to respond to their demands, but eventually it became supportive (Sprinzak, 1991: 46–47).

It was after the Yom Kippur War in 1973 that the settlement enterprise gathered momentum. This was largely due to the establishment of Gush Emunim ("the Bloc of the Faithful") in 1974, an organization dedicated to building Jewish settlements on the land conquered in the Six-Day War. This organization was highly successful. It worked tirelessly and skillfully to convince successive Israel governments to found settlements and entice Jews to live in them. These efforts were not without setbacks. For instance, the Sinai Peninsula was returned to Egypt in 1979, and Gaza was given over to its Palestinian inhabitants in 2005, even though Jewish settlements had been established in these locations. Still, the settlement enterprise continued, particularly in the West Bank. As noted already, half a million Jewish settlers live in these settlements at present, and they continue to grow in number and size (Sprinzak, 1991: 65–67, 107–66).

What is extraordinary is that the religious Zionists have never constituted more than 10 percent of the Israeli population, but they were able to persuade one Israeli government after another to support their aims through savvy political maneuvering and the passion of their vision. That vision seemed to move even secular Israelis. By the 1970s, the idealism that had inspired secular Zionism began to wane as Israel became wealthier and began to enjoy a relatively high standard of living. Secular Israelis therefore admired the young religious pioneers who set out to settle the territories conquered in the Six-Day War. These people reminded secular Israelis of the idealism that they themselves once had (Gorenberg, 2006).

Despite the embrace of a violent theology by R. Tsevi Yehudah Kook and his followers, the settlement enterprise has not resulted in much overt violence on the part of the settlers against Palestinians. Instances of such violence have been sporadic, limited in scope, and often directed at Palestinian property. Most of the violence between the two groups has come from the Palestinian side. The most salient examples were the two Intifadas in 1987–93 and 2000–5. Yet the fact that Palestinians have been more violent here is due to the fact that the settlers have had no real need to initiate violence, given that they are in the superior position. The Israeli army has exercised tight military control over the areas in which the settlements have been established and it has protected them and their inhabitants.

Yet one could argue that Israel's military rule over Palestinians in the West Bank and its support of the settlement enterprise constitute violence against Palestinians of the "structural" kind. As I noted in my introductory section, structural violence involves one group oppressing another politically, socially, or economically. The harm done here is more subtle than with overt violence in that the damage is done physically and psychologically over an extended period of time, but it is violence nonetheless and in the long run can be just as harmful as violence in which there is actual bloodshed. Israel's behavior toward the Palestinians in the West Bank qualifies as structural violence. Depriving Palestinians of their basic human rights and the appropriation of Palestinian land for the building of settlements is certainly violence of this kind (Eisen, 2011: 12, 14, 166–67).

In addition, some instances of more direct forms of violence perpetrated by religious Zionists are among the most notorious instances of political violence in Israel's history. One such instance was the massacre in 1994 of twenty-nine Palestinians in the Cave of the Patriarchs in Hebron by Baruch Goldstein. More notorious was the assassination of the Israeli prime minister, Yitzhak Rabin, who was gunned down in 1995 by Yigal Amir. Both these instances of violence were prompted by the signing of the Oslo Accords in 1993, an agreement that provided a framework for resolving the Middle East conflict by proposing the creation of a Palestinian state in the West Bank and Gaza. Most religious Zionists were vehemently opposed to the accords because, in their thinking, they represented a reversal of the messianic process. Religious Zionists therefore pledged to do everything in their power to stop them from taking effect.

It is important to keep in mind that Goldstein and Amir were lone wolves who received no official sanction from religious Zionist rabbis to use violence for this purpose. Most religious Zionists who opposed the Oslo Accords did so through nonviolent means: protest, government lobbying, and submitting court petitions. Still, the violent actions of Goldstein and Amir were remarkably successful. The political and social turmoil that was created in Israel because of what they did – particularly the assassination of Rabin – eventually derailed the peace process (Sprinzak, 1999: chapters 7–8).

After the death of R. Tsevi Yehudah Kook, his disciples attempted to carry on his legacy, but they branched out in a number of different directions. This fragmentation, in fact, was already evident in the later years of R. Tsevi Yehudah's life. Israel's ever-changing and complex political landscape and the constant shifts in Israeli attitudes to the peace process prompted widely different theological explanations among R. Tsevi Yehudah's students. There were also rabbis and thinkers affiliated with religious Zionism who were never followers of R. Tsevi Yehudah, and they added to the variety of opinion in the religious Zionist community (Holzer, 2009: 230–76; Inbari, 2012).

Some of R. Tsevi Yehudah's disciples became more militant than their teacher. Several of them, for instance, developed violent and xenophobic views regarding the Middle East conflict that drew from Kabbalistic sources. They believed that the nations of the world were agents of metaphysical forces of evil, while the Jews were agents of metaphysical forces of good, and it was for this reason that the state of Israel was under constant siege by the Palestinians and the surrounding Arab countries. The forces of evil were determined to quash the forces of good so that the messianic redemption would not proceed. Others among R. Tsevi Yehudah's militant disciples spoke in favor of waging unprovoked war against the neighboring Arab countries. If the messianic redemption was indeed unfolding, Jews should take the initiative and grab more land that would belong to the future messianic kingdom. Jews did not have to wait for the Arabs to initiate a war with Israel to take such action, nor did Jews have to worry about international opinion, given that God was on their side (Ravitzky, 1996: 83–84; Holzer, 2009: 230–36, 249–56).

These ideas, however, did not go unchallenged. Some of R. Tsevi Yehudah's more moderate students rejected them. Some, in fact, were so alarmed by the increasingly militant tone of their colleagues that they began to distance themselves from R. Tsevi Yehudah's followers. Challenges to the militant views of R. Tsevi Yehudah's students also came from representatives of religious Zionism who had never been among his followers to begin with (Holzer, 2009: 249–76).

At present, religious Zionism in all its variety still represents a small sector of Israeli society, but its adherents' influence on Israeli politics is significant and likely to continue, and not just because of the settlement enterprise or the actions of their most militant individuals. As mentioned in my introductory section, religious Zionists serve in the Israeli army in numbers disproportionate to other subgroups in the Israeli population, and this disproportion is even greater in the officer corps. The army is central in Israeli society, and therefore the overrepresentation of religious Zionists in the army will ensure that they have a prominent place in that society for some time to come.

5.4 Conclusions

One does not necessarily need to refer to religion to explain why Jews have become violent in the modern period. Prior to that era, Jews had been subjugated by one nation after another for more than two and a half millennia, and they lived most of that time in exile from their homeland. Zionism provided Jews a way out of this situation; and because of their long history of suffering, it was perhaps inevitable that they were willing to engage in violence to ensure that Zionism succeeded.

Social Identity Theory (SIT) sheds light on this. It tells us that groups under stress will attempt to preserve their identity by adopting xenophobic views that may in turn inspire violence. Well, Jews have had a record of stress that is unmatched in the annals of world history both in terms of its duration and intensity. Their history is punctuated by trauma, the worst being the Holocaust, and even when Jews were not experiencing trauma, their lives were characterized by constant humiliation as a people ruled by others who were hostile to them. Therefore, it is understandable that Jews would turn to violence to ensure the success of the Zionist enterprise. Those who supported this enterprise saw it as the only hope that Jews had of surviving as a people.

Yet even if one does not need religion to explain such violence, the question is whether religion still played a role in its instigation, and our discussion in this section has argued that it did. Judaism gave Zionists a framework for their aspirations to create a modern Jewish state in which Jews would be free of the oppression and humiliation of the exile, and it also helped justify the need for violence to make these aspirations a reality.

This assessment is most evident in religious Zionism. Here, the aspirations of Zionism for building a modern Jewish state were explicitly equated with messianism. Zionism was evidence that the end of history was at hand and that Jews would be rescued from their suffering. To justify the equation of Zionism with messianism, R. Abraham Isaac Kook formulated a theology based on sources in the rabbinic tradition that espoused an active messianism. According to his vision, the messianic period would evolve gradually through the normal course of historical events, and human beings would therefore be participants in bringing the messianic process to completion, not just bystanders.

Eventually, this understanding of Zionism justified violence as well. We have seen in earlier sections that messianism could lead to violence because it contained the idea that God would wage war on the oppressors of the Jewish people as he redeemed them, and it was therefore a short step from this idea to the notion that Jews should help the redemption process along by using violence against their enemies. That, in fact, was the position that some Jews adopted in the two rebellions against Rome in the first and second centuries CE. We saw that, because of the disastrous outcome of the two rebellions, rabbinic Judaism opposed this way of thinking and therefore attempted to quell messianism and its violent tendencies. Yet the potential for violence that was inherent in Jewish messianism was never extirpated by the rabbis, and religious Zionism essentially revived this element of messianism and developed it. R. Kook himself rejected violence as part of his active messianism, but his son and his son's disciples did not. For R. Tsevi Yehudah Kook, violence was a legitimate part of messianic activism and was necessary for completing the messianic process.

Interestingly, Jewish sources may also help explain the violence of secular Zionism. A small minority of militant secular Zionists explicitly drew from the Bible to justify violence. However, the more moderate secular Zionists who made up the bulk of the Zionist movement may have also been motivated to use violence by Jewish sources, even if they did not explicitly cite them. It is possible that secular Zionism was, in essence, a secularized version of Jewish messianism, and thus, in absorbing Jewish messianism, secular Zionism may have absorbed its violent features as well.

The connection between Jewish messianism and the violence of secular Zionism is speculative in relying on judgments about subconscious forces. Most secular Zionists saw the violence they engaged in as simple self-defense. Still, this connection cannot be ruled out. Moreover, if secular Zionists viewed their violent actions as defensive, that view may have also had religious roots, given that the right to act in self-defense is one of Judaism's most time-honored ethical principles.

6 Conclusions

In this final section, I will summarize and consolidate the lessons we have learned in the previous sections. I will also speculate about what these lessons mean for the future.

Our summary begins with the Bible, which provided the foundational concepts for Jewish attitudes on violence in subsequent Jewish history. The Bible espoused a theology of history that was formulated in the kingdom of Judah in ancient Israel over a period of several centuries when the Judeans were threatened, attacked, and subjugated by larger empires. This theology helped the Judeans survive their difficult circumstances because it convinced them that the one true God was on their side and that he would help them defeat their enemies so long as they observed his commandments. However, the same theology also injected violent elements into the biblical text. The difficult situation of the Judeans prompted biblical writers to project aggressive forms of violence toward non-Jews onto the imagined past and the imagined future. According to these writers, the Israelites had originally taken possession of their land because they had conquered and annihilated its prior inhabitants with God's encouragement and assistance. The same writers also predicted that, in the future, when the Israelites and Judeans returned to their land after the exile, God would take vengeance on their oppressors.

The biblical theology of history was adopted by the rabbis who gradually emerged as the authoritative religious leaders of the Jewish community in the wake of the destruction of the Jewish state in the first century CE. The rabbis also refined this theology with the help of material from outside the biblical text. According to the rabbis, the loss of Jewish independence was because of the sins of the Jews, and it marked the beginning of the exile predicted in the Bible. Yet the rabbis also held fast to the biblical promise that the exile would eventually come to an end with the advent of the messianic era and that God would punish the nations that had oppressed his people.

This biblical-rabbinic theology of history remained fundamental to Judaism in the medieval and early modern periods, but it underwent further development in Kabbalah. The Kabbalists recast this theology in dramatic cosmic terms. The world was divided between metaphysical forces of good represented by the Jews and metaphysical forces of evil represented by the non-Jewish nations of the world, and this paradigm explained why the Jews were in exile; the forces of evil were ascendant. However, the forces of good would eventually triumph, and this victory would manifest itself on earth with the advent of the messianic era.

The aspect of the biblical-rabbinic theology of history that was most important for our purposes was that concerned with the messianic era because it had the most significant implications for Jewish violence in subsequent history. A consistent feature of this theology was that God would punish the nations that had tormented the Jews. This idea did not necessarily encourage Jews to engage in violence against non-Jews; it was God who would punish the non-Jewish nations who had oppressed them, not the Jews themselves, and this punishment would take place only in the messianic era. However, if Jews were subjugated to another nation and were convinced that the messianic era was near, it was not going to take much imagination for them to conclude that they should help God bring about their redemption by engaging in violent action against their overlords. In fact, some Jews in the first centuries CE adopted this way of thinking and therefore rebelled twice against Roman rule. However, both rebellions had disastrous results, and as a result, the rabbis did their best to take the focus away from messianism. Nonetheless, the rabbis did not reject messianism in principle nor the belief that the messianic era would be accompanied by violence; they kept these ideas alive, and Kabbalah developed them even further. Thus, the potential for messianism to incite Jews to violence against their enemies was maintained as well.

It was not until the modern period, almost two millennia after the beginning of the exile, that this potential was once again activated among Jews. The Zionist movement was founded on the premise that Jews should return to their homeland and build their own state so that they would no longer be victim to the seemingly incurable hatred that the non-Jewish world had toward them. Even though this movement was mostly secular, it aroused messianic longings among some Orthodox Jews, and these Jews came to believe that Zionism represented the unfolding of the messianic process. Eventually, these Zionists concluded, as did Jews in the first two centuries CE, that violence was a legitimate means to move this process along.

Yet Jewish messianism may have also affected secular Zionism. Secular Zionists no longer believed in the biblical-rabbinic theology of history, but their thinking may have still been based, at least in part, on Jewish messianism in secular form. Moreover, because Jewish messianism involved violent vengeance against the nations that had oppressed the Jews, it is plausible that the willingness of secular Zionists to engage in violence for their cause had roots in Jewish messianism as well. Some secular Zionists were also inspired by the two rebellions against Roman rule in the first two centuries that were motivated by messianic beliefs, even if these Zionists did not explicitly share those beliefs.

For right-wing secular Zionists, the messianic idea was not the only Jewish source for their embrace of violence, nor necessarily the most important. These Zionists admired the military initiatives of the Israelites throughout the biblical history and found inspiration in them for an unapologetic muscular Zionism.

As I have said repeatedly, whether the violence perpetrated by the Zionist movement was justified is an issue that should not sidetrack us. What is important for our concerns is that, with the advent of Zionism, Jews have engaged in violence against non-Jews on a national scale for the first time in almost two thousand years, and some of the inspiration for that violence has religious roots. There is far more certainty that this has been the case with religious Zionism than with secular Zionism. Still, the latter possibility must not be discounted. Furthermore, religious Zionism, despite its small numbers, has had an enormous impact on the Middle East conflict. Therefore, the connection between Judaism and violence looms large in this conflict, even if it is manifested in religious Zionism alone.

6.1 Social Identity Theory

Our analysis throughout this book was aided by insights from social psychology – in particular, Social Identity Theory (SIT). SIT has shown that social identity is closely tied to an individual's sense of self-esteem and is therefore critical for human well-being. It also teaches us how groups can become violent with little provocation. A group can become violent when it experiences any pressure that threatens the self-esteem of its constituents. Jews have experienced such pressures, both physical and psychological, throughout their long history, and at times those pressures have been immense. However, Jews, as a people, have not had the capacity to act violently in response to those pressures except in the periods of ancient and modern Israel, periods in which Jews have had political power. For a good portion of their history, Jews were unable to engage in collective violence because they were under the domination of others. Still, even in this part of their history, Jews fantasized about violence by believing that their oppressors would eventually be punished by God, and this idea kept the potential of Jewish violence alive until the creation of the modern state of Israel.

The insights of Vamik Volkan were also helpful for our purposes. Volkan has highlighted the important role that "chosen traumas" play in inspiring ethnic and national groups to be violent. These traumas often function as focal points for ethnic and national identity, and when they remain unhealed, they can become a rallying cry for violence. Jews provide an excellent example of this phenomenon. They have suffered more traumas throughout their history than any other people, they commemorate those traumas on a regular basis, and, for this reason, they are prone to lash out violently against any and all threats, real or perceived.

6.2 The Future

What about the future? If the creation of the state of Israel has motivated Jews to engage in violence, will Jews continue to do so, and, if so, to what extent will that violence be motivated by religion?

Let us begin with the first question: Will Jews continue to engage in violence on behalf of Israel? All signs indicate that they will, both on the domestic and on the international fronts. On the domestic front, the West Bank is a powder keg that could explode at any time. Israel continues to rule over the West Bank, and religious Zionists continue to build settlements there. The Palestinians in the West Bank number in the millions, they deeply resent Israeli rule and the growth of settlements, and they could therefore rebel at any time as they have in the past. If they do, Israel will likely respond with violence as they have done in the past. The United States and other powers have attempted on several occasions to broker a peace deal between the two sides that would establish an independent Palestinian state in the West Bank and Gaza, but all such efforts have failed. As usual, Israelis and Palestinians have different narratives about these failures, with each group claiming justice for their side. Yet regardless of which narrative one subscribes to, the important point is that, in the future, Israelis and Palestinians will likely be drawn into more violent confrontations in the West Bank.

On the international front, Israel is likely to be drawn into more violent confrontations as well. Iran has become Israel's major international adversary. Iran's leaders speak openly about their desire to destroy Israel. Iran also supports Hezbollah, a proxy militia in Lebanon that threatens Israel on its northern border. Iranian troops are also stationed in Syria, which shares Israel's northeastern border, and they too pose a threat to Israel. Hamas, which governs in Gaza, is also sworn to Israel's destruction, and it sends rockets into Israel on a frequent basis. In recent years, violence has erupted frequently between Israel and these adversaries, and, in all likelihood, this violence will continue. It may also develop into an all-out war on one or more of the borders that Israel shares with them.

There is an irony in Israel's situation. Jews escaped subjugation by other nations to build a state in their ancient homeland, a state that they hoped would give them security both physically and psychologically. Yet not only has Israel failed to make them secure; it may have made them feel even *less* secure. Almost half of the world's Jewish population now resides in Israel, a tiny state the size of New Jersey. Such a concentration of Jews in one small area surrounded by enemies has arguably made them more vulnerable to their enemies than at any time in history since their exile in the first century CE.

If Jews continue to engage in violence for the state of Israel, to what extent will that violence remain rooted in religion? Obviously, religious Zionists will continue to fight on behalf of Israel for religious reasons, and the fact they are represented disproportionately in the Israeli army will give them ample opportunity to do so. Moreover, religious Zionists are likely to continue to build settlements in the West Bank for religious reasons, and again it can be argued that this activity is violence in the structural sense. However, it is harder to say where secular Israelis stand on this question. Secular Jews in Israel have become increasingly disconnected from the earlier idealism that once captivated them, and they have therefore become increasingly disconnected from the religious roots that may have unconsciously informed secular Zionism. At the same time, though, secular Israelis in recent years have become more interested in religion in their daily lives on a conscious level. Most have not become Orthodox, but they have embraced more elements of Jewish practice and ritual than they once did (Pew, 2016). It is hard to say where this trend is going. It is also difficult to predict how it will affect attitudes to violence, if at all.

Are there insights in this Element that may help provide a solution to the Middle East conflict? Even if this conflict is likely to continue for the foreseeable future, we can still speculate on the basis of what we have learned in the previous pages about what may bring Jews closer to making peace with their adversaries. Of course, peace will not arrive until *both* sides of the Middle East conflict are willing to make peace, but because this Element has been focused on Jews, I will deal with their side alone.

I can think of two courses of action that could help Jews be more receptive to peace. The first involves the non-Jewish world. The major reason that Jews adopted Zionism in the first place was that they felt under siege. They saw no hope for Jewish life in Europe because of its seemingly incurable antisemitism, and they therefore felt that they had no choice but to return to their homeland and use violence if necessary for that purpose. Jews will continue to use violence in the Middle East for the same reasons. As long as Jews believe that they under siege, they will feel that they have no choice but to do so; and the fact of the matter is that Jews do, in fact, remain under siege. Large number of Palestinians, Arabs, and Muslims speak openly about wanting to see an end to the state of Israel. Their rhetoric is also filled with antisemitic tropes that reflect a hatred of Jews everywhere, not just Israelis. Moreover, in recent years, antisemitism has made a return in Western countries. The antisemitic rhetoric of Palestinians, Arabs, and Muslims finds a peculiar resonance with similar rhetoric being used in the West on the extreme right and left. If one argues that these threats usually take the form of mere words and that Jews are overreacting, one has to remember that words mean a great deal to Jews. A German dictator not long ago threatened Jews with words and ended up killing 6 million of them. One also has to remember what SIT teaches us. It does not take much to provoke a people into violence when they feel threatened, especially a people such as the Jews who have suffered so much throughout history.

So what may help bring a solution to the Middle East conflict is for the world to recognize the damaging effects of the constant threats against Israel and the ugly antisemitism that has lately become so widespread. The world also needs to actively combat these problems. The more talk there is of destroying Israel or that Jews are evil, the more Jews will stiffen their resolve to defend their state with the use of violence at all costs.

I fully realize that Israel does plenty that is open to criticism. I recognize that Israel is in part to blame for the fact that the Middle East conflict has not been resolved. Yet I also believe that Israel and its Jewish supporters will be far more pliable, far more willing to participate in a peace process, if they believe that the world is truly sympathetic to them and their concerns. As things stand now, many Jews do not feel that way. The rampant and hateful rhetoric against Israel and Jews and the lack of resolve on the part of the world as a whole to combat it have made it very difficult for Jews to let go of the notion that the non-Jewish world will only do them harm, and that has in turn made it difficult for Jews to conceive of Israel making peace with its enemies.

However, the onus of creating more favorable conditions for ending the Middle East conflict does not fall just on non-Jews, and this leads to the second course of action that I believe may help resolve the conflict. Jews themselves must take initiative here. They must recognize the injustices that Israel has committed against Palestinians, and they must make every effort to rectify those injustices. Even if Jews are not ready to give Palestinians their own state, they can do much more to alleviate Palestinian suffering.

Jews should also avail themselves of a wealth of resources in their religious tradition that support peace. The subject matter of this Element has been Judaism and violence, and therefore it has dwelled on texts and ideas in Judaism that have led to violence. Yet it is important to emphasize, as I did in my introductory section, that there are just as many texts and ideas in Judaism that encourage peaceful behavior, and Jews should therefore be active in seeking inspiration from these resources, not just those that encourage violence.

A brief summary of some of the Jewish texts and ideas that encourage peaceful behavior will give some indication of how rich this dimension of Judaism is. Many of the Jewish sources we have explored in this Element that encourage violence against non-Jews are rooted in negative views of them. Yet there are other Jewish sources that view non-Jews in a far more positive way. In the first chapter of the Hebrew Bible, we are told that human beings are created in the image of God, an idea that suggests that all people are exalted in God's eyes, not just Jews. Sources in rabbinic Judaism offer a similar message. In one Talmudic passage, we are told that God created the human race from a single individual so that no person could say "my father is greater than yours" (Mishnah, *Sanhedrin* 4:5). This dictum implies equality between Jews and non-Jews in that they are all descended from a common ancestor. As we have noted in Section 4, in the medieval period there were schools of Jewish philosophy that attempted to understand Judaism in a rational manner, and these schools tended to view non-Jews in a strikingly more positive way than the rival schools of Kabbalah did. In the modern period, liberal forms of Judaism have expressed views on non-Jews that are more positive than any in Jewish history. One of the central ideas of Reform Judaism is that all human beings are beloved by God and that the mission of Jews is to work together with non-Jews to create a better world.

There are also many Jewish sources that encourage Jews not only to view non-Jews positively but to behave kindly toward them as well. Perhaps most famous in this regard is the biblical command, "love your neighbor as yourself" (Lev. 19:18). In several other biblical passages, one finds a remarkably positive attitude toward foreigners who have chosen to reside in the land of Israel while retaining their foreign identity. The Israelites are commanded to love them and protect them (Ex. 22:20; Deut. 10:19, 24:17–22).

In rabbinic Judaism, there are also numerous sources that encourage Jews to treat non-Jews benevolently. In one rabbinic passage, Abaye, a Babylonian rabbi, says that a person should always strive to be on peaceful terms with others, including non-Jews, so as to be beloved by God and all fellow human beings (Babylonian Talmud, *Berakhot* 17a). Most important are a series of special decrees that were instituted by the rabbis "on account of the paths of peace" (*mipney darkey shalom*). These decrees were meant to create a more peaceful world, and some of them involved non-Jews. Thus, Jews must give charity to non-Jews, visit their sick, and bury their dead (Mishnah, *Gittin* 5:8–9; Babylonian Talmud, *Gittin* 61a, 62a).

Closer to the heart of the concerns of this Element is that some Jewish sources are clearly uncomfortable with violence toward non-Jews or oppose it altogether. Scholars have noted that, for instance, in the Bible, the books of 1 and 2 Chronicles retell the biblical history in a manner that clearly mutes the violence of Israel's wars described in the historical books of the Prophets (Niditch, 1993: 132–33, 139–41, 149). In chapter 3 of this book, we saw that the rabbis, on the whole, discouraged Jews from engaging in such violence against their Roman oppressors. We speculated that the rabbis may have done so for pragmatic reasons, but we did not exclude the possibility that the rabbis were motivated by moral concerns as well.

Most important is that, in the modern period, Zionism has always included factions that have been devoted to making peace with Palestinians, have supported far-reaching concessions for that purpose, and have based their thinking in whole or in part on religious principles. The most prominent of these in early Zionism was *Berit Shalom* ("Covenant of Peace"), which was established in 1925. Its leadership was made up of leading Jewish intellectuals in Palestine. Central to their platform was the belief that Jews and Arabs in Palestine should join together to form a binational state in which the two groups would have equal rights regardless of which of them was in the majority. *Berit Shalom* eventually disbanded and many of its members later founded *Ihud* (Unity), the platform of which was similar to that of *Berit Shalom*. Neither *Berit Shalom* nor *Ihud* won much popular support, but they were nonetheless influential because of the prominence of their leaders. Moreover, their legacy has been carried on by peace groups that have arisen in Israel since its creation. These groups have mostly supported a two-state solution, according to which a Palestinian state would be created in the West Bank and Gaza (Bar-On, 1996).

These groups, by and large, have been secular in orientation, but even religious Zionism has produced factions in favor of a peace settlement with Palestinians based on a two-state solution. As noted in the previous section, R. Abraham Isaac Kook himself, the forefather of messianic religious Zionism, insisted that Zionism should not involve the shedding of blood. After the Six-Day War, religious Zionism took a more militant turn due to the influence of R. Kook's son, R. Tsevi Yehudah Kook, but not all religious Zionists approved of the new direction. A vocal minority strongly opposed it, and in the 1970s and 1980s, they established several organizations favoring concessions to the Palestinians. The most notable of these were *'Oz ve-Shalom / Netivot Shalom* and *Meimad* (Bar-On, 1996).

This summary of the peaceful dimension of Judaism is only the tip of the iceberg. There are many other sources that can be called on to demonstrate how rich this dimension of Judaism is (Eisen, 2011). Jews therefore have ample resources within Judaism to counterbalance its violent aspects and construct a Judaism that encourages peace. Some Jewish thinkers and scholars have already done a great deal of work on this issue. For instance, there are initiatives being conducted today in which religious Zionist rabbis and sheikhs in the Islamic Movement in Israel have been working together to advance peace and to find ways to interpret their respective sacred texts in a peaceful vein (Melchior, 2018). However, more work needs to be done, and Jews will have to support such efforts in greater numbers for them to succeed.

References

Adwan, S. D., Bar-On, D., & Naveh, E., eds. (2012). *Side by Side: Parallel Histories of Israel-Palestine*, New York: Peace Research Institute in the Middle East.

Appleby, R. S. (2000). *The Ambivalence of the Sacred: Religion, Violence, and Reconciliation*, Lanham, MD: Rowman & Littlefield Publishers.

Avot de-Rabi Natan (1967). ed. S. Schechter, New York: Feldheim.

Bar-On, M. (1996). *In Pursuit of Peace: A History of the Israeli Peace Movement*, Washington, DC: The United States Institute of Peace.

Beiser, F. C. (2018). *Hermann Cohen: An Intellectual Biography*, Oxford, Oxford University Press.

Berger, M. S. (2007). Taming the Beast: Rabbinic Pacification of Second-Century Jewish Nationalism. In J. K. Wellman, Jr., ed., *Belief and Bloodshed: Religion and Violence across Time and Tradition*, Lanham, MD: Rowman & Littlefield Publishers, pp. 47–62.

Biale, D. (2011). *Not in the Heavens: The Tradition of Jewish Secular Thought*, Princeton, NJ: Princeton University Press.

Boyarin, D. (1997). *Unheroic Conduct: The Rise of Heterosexuality and the Invention of the Jewish Man*, Berkeley: University of California Press.

Brett, M. G. (1995). Nationalism and the Hebrew Bible. In J. W. Rogerson, M. Davies, & M. D. Caroll R., eds., *The Bible in Ethics*, Sheffield: Sheffield Academic Press, pp. 136–63.

Cohen, G. D. (1991). Esau As Symbol in Early Medieval Thought. In *Studies in the Variety of Rabbinic Cultures*, Philadelphia: The Jewish Publication Society of America, pp. 243–69.

Collins, J. J. (2010). *The Scepter and the Star: Messianism in Light of the Dead Sea Scrolls*, 2nd ed., Grand Rapids, MI and Cambridge: William B. Eerdmans Publishing.

Cross, F. M. (1973). *Canaanite Myth and Hebrew Epic*, Cambridge, MA: Harvard University Press.

DellaPergola, S. (2001). Some Fundamentals of Jewish Demographic History. In S. DellaPergola & J. Even, eds., *Papers in Jewish Demography 1997*, Jerusalem: Avraham Harman Institute of Contemporary Jewry, Hebrew University of Jerusalem, World Union of Jewish Studies, Association for Jewish Demography and Statistics, pp. 11–33.

Demmers, J. (2017). *Theories of Conflict*, 2nd ed., London: Routledge.

Efron, J., Weitzman, S., & Lehmann, M. (2013). *The Jews: A History*, 2nd ed., London and New York: Routledge.

Eisen, R. (2011). *The Peace and Violence of Judaism: From the Bible to Modern Zionism*, New York: Oxford University Press.

Eliade, M. (1971). *The Myth of the Eternal Return: Or, Cosmos and History*, Princeton, NJ: Princeton University Press.

Galtung, J. (1990). Cultural Violence. *Journal of Peace Research* 27(3), 291–305.

Goldenberg, R. (2006). The Destruction of the Temple: Its Meaning and Consequences. In S. T. Katz, ed., *The Cambridge History of Judaism, Volume 4: The Late Roman-Rabbinic Period*, Cambridge: Cambridge University Press, pp. 191–205.

Gorenberg, G. (2006). *The Accidental Empire: Israel and the Birth of the Settlements, 1967–1977*, New York: Times Books.

Greenberg, M. (1995). Mankind, Israel, and the Nations in the Hebraic Heritage. In *Studies in the Bible and Jewish Thought*, Philadelphia: The Jewish Publication Society of America, pp. 369–93.

Hillers, D. (1969). *Covenant: The History of a Biblical Idea*, Baltimore, MD: Johns Hopkins University Press.

Hogg, M. A. (2016). Social Identity Theory. In S. McKeown, R. Haji, & N. Ferguson, eds., *Understanding Peace and Conflict through Social Identity Theory*, New York: Springer, pp. 3–18.

Holzer, E. (2009). *A Double-Edged Sword: Military Activism in the Thought of Religious Zionism [in Hebrew]*, Jerusalem: The Hartman Institute.

Horsley, R. A. (1992). "Messianic" Figures and Movements in First-Century Palestine. In J. H. Charlesworth, ed., *The Messiah: Developments in Earliest Judaism and Christianity*, Minneapolis: Fortress, pp. 276–95.

Inbari, M. (2012). *Messianic Religious Zionism Confronts Territorial Compromises*, Cambridge: Cambridge University Press.

Jaffee, M. S. (2006). *Early Judaism: Religious Worlds of the First Judaic Millennium*, 2nd ed., Bethesda: University Press of Maryland.

Kaminsky, J. S. (2007). *Yet I Loved Jacob: Reclaiming the Biblical Concept of Election*, Nashville, TN: Abingdon Press.

Kellner, M. (1991). *Maimonides on Judaism and the Jewish People*, Albany: State University of New York Press.

Kimelman, R. (2006). Rabbinic Prayer in Late Antiquity. In S. T. Katz, ed., *The Cambridge History of Judaism, Volume 4: The Late Roman-Rabbinic Period*, Cambridge: Cambridge University Press, pp. 573–611.

Krug, E. G., Dahlberg, L. L., Mercy, J. A., Zwi, A. B., & Lozano, R. (2002). *World Report on Violence and Health*, Geneva: World Health Organization.

Liberles, R. (1995). *Salo Wittmayer Baron: Architect of Jewish History*, New York: New York University Press.

Lüders, A., Jonas, E., Fristche, I. & Agroskin, D. (2016). Between the Lines of Us and Them: Identity Threat, Anxious Uncertainty, and Reactive In-Group Affirmation: How Can Anti-Social Outcomes be Prevented? In S. McKeown, R. Haji, & N. Ferguson, eds., *Understanding Peace and Conflict through Social Identity Theory*, New York: Springer, pp. 33–54.

Luz, E. (2003). *Wrestling with an Angel: Power, Morality, and Jewish Identity*, trans. M. Swirsky, New Haven, CT: Yale University Press.

Mandel,M. (2009). Assimilation and Cultural Exchange in Modern Jewish History. In J. Cohen & M. Rosman, eds., *Rethinking European Jewish History*, Oxford and Portland, OR: The Littman Library of Jewish Civilization, pp. 72–92.

Marks, R. G. (1994). *The Image of Bar Kokhba in Traditional Jewish Literature: False Messiah and National Hero*, University Park: Pennsylvania State University Press.

Mavor, K. I. & Ysseldyk, R. (2020). A Social Identity Approach to Religion. In K. E. Vail III & Clay Routledge, eds., *The Science, Religion, and Spirituality of Existentialism*, London: Academic Press, pp. 187–205.

Melchior, M. (2018). Opening the Tent of Peace. In G. Overland et al., eds., *Violent Extremism in the 21st Century*, Cambridge: Cambridge Scholars Publishing, pp. 447–52.

Meyer, M. A. (1988). *Response to Modernity: A History of the Reform Movement in Judaism*, New York: Oxford University Press.

Myers, J. (1991). The Messianic Idea and Zionist Ideologies. In Jonathan Frankel, ed., *Studies in Contemporary Jewry, Volume 7: Jews and Messianism in the Modern Era: Metaphor and Meaning*, New York: Oxford University Press, pp. 3–13.

Niditch, S. (1993). *War in the Hebrew Bible: A Study in the Ethics of Violence*, New York: Oxford University Press.

Pew Research Center (2016). "Israel's Religiously-Divided Society," www .pewforum.org/2016/03/08/israels-religiously-divided-society/.

Ravitzky, A. (1996). *Messianism, Zionism, and Jewish Religious Radicalism*, trans. M. Swirsky & J. Chipman, Chicago: University of Chicago Press.

Ross, M. H. (1993). *The Culture of Conflict: Interpretations and Interests in Comparative Perspective*, New Haven, CT: Yale University Press.

Rowlett, L. (1996). *Joshua and the Rhetoric of Violence: A New Historicist Analysis*, Sheffield: Sheffield Academic Press.

Sagi, A. (1994). The Punishment of Amalek in Jewish Tradition: Coping with the Moral Problem. *Harvard Theological Review* 87(5), 323–46.

Schiffman, L. (2006). Messianism and Apocalypticism in Rabbinic Texts. In S. T. Katz, ed., *The Cambridge History of Judaism, Volume 4: The Late Roman-Rabbinic Period*, Cambridge: Cambridge University Press, pp. 1053–72.

Scholem, G. (1971). Toward an Understanding of the Messianic Idea in Judaism. In G. Scholem, *The Messianic Idea in Judaism and Other Essays on Jewish Spirituality*, New York: Schocken Books, pp. 1–36.

Seul, J. R. (1999). "Ours Is the Way of God": Religion, Identity, and Intergroup Conflict. *Journal of Peace Research* 36(5), 553–69.

Shapira, A. (1992). *Land and Power: The Zionist Resort to Force, 1881–1948*, trans. W. Templer, New York: Oxford University Press.

Shimoni, G. (1995). *The Zionist Ideology*, Waltham, MA: Brandeis University Press.

Smith, M. S. (2001). *The Origins of Biblical Monotheism: Israel's Polytheistic Background and the Ugaritic Texts*, New York: Oxford University Press.

Sprinzak, E. (1991). *The Ascendance of Israel's Radical Right*, New York: Oxford.

Sprinzak, E. (1999). *Brother Against Brother: Violence and Extremism in Israeli Politics from the Altalena to the Rabin Assassination*, New York: Adama Books.

Tigay, J. H. (2003). *The JPS Commentary on the Torah: Deuteronomy*, 2nd ed., Philadelphia: The Jewish Publication Society of America.

Tishby, I. (1989). *The Wisdom of the Zohar*, vol. 1, trans. D. Goldstein, Oxford: Oxford University Press.

Volkan, V. D. (2007). Massive Trauma: The Political Ideology of Entitlement and Violence. *Revue Française de Psychanalyse* 74(4), 1047–59.

Wills, L. M. D. (2014). In A. Berlin & M. Z. Brettler, eds., *The Jewish Study Bible*, New York: Oxford University Press, pp. 1635–37.

Wolfson, E. R. (2006). *Venturing Beyond: Law and Morality in Kabbalistic Mysticism*, New York: Oxford University Press.

Ysseldyk, R., Matheson, K., & Anisman, H. (2010). Religion As Identity: Toward an Understanding of Religion from a Social Identity Perspective. *Personality and Social Psychology Review* 14(1), 60–71.

Acknowledgments

I would like to thank a number of individuals who helped make this Element possible. The first is Margo Kitts who invited me to write it. I would also like to thank my colleagues Motti Inbari and Daniel Roth who reviewed the manuscript and offered invaluable suggestions for improving it. I would also like to thank Christopher Rollston for doing the same for the section on the Hebrew Bible. Needless to say, any remaining errors in this Element are my own responsibility.

Cambridge Elements $\equiv$

Religion and Violence

James R. Lewis
Wuhan University

James R. Lewis is Professor at Wuhan University, and the
author and editor of a number of volumes, including *The
Cambridge Companion to Religion and Terrorism*.

Margo Kitts
Hawai'i Pacific University

Margo Kitts edits the *Journal of Religion and Violence* and is
Professor and Coordinator of Religious Studies and East-West
Classical Studies at Hawai'i Pacific University in Honolulu.

ABOUT THE SERIES

Violence motivated by religious beliefs has become all too common
in the years since the 9/11 attacks. Not surprisingly, interest in the
topic of religion and violence has grown substantially since then.
This Elements series on Religion and Violence addresses this new,
frontier topic in a series of ca. fifty individual Elements. Collectively,
the volumes will examine a range of topics, including violence in
major world religious traditions, theories of religion and violence,
holy war, witch hunting, and human sacrifice, among others.

Cambridge Elements ≡

Religion and Violence

ELEMENTS IN THE SERIES

Religious Culture and Violence in Traditional China
Barend ter Haar

Mormonism and Violence: The Battles of Zion
Patrick Q. Mason

Islam and Suicide Attacks
Pieter Nanninga

Tibetan Demonology
Christopher Bell

Religious Terrorism
Heather S. Gregg

The Bahá'í Faith, Violence, and Non-Violence
Robert H. Stockman

Great War, Religious Dimensions
Bobby Wintermute

Transforming the Sacred into Saintliness: Reflecting on Violence and Religion with René Girard
Wolfgang Palaver

Christianity and Violence
Lloyd Steffen

Violated and Transcended Bodies: Gender, Martyrdom, and Asceticism in Early Christianity
Gail P. Streete

Lone Wolf Race Warriors and White Genocide
Mattias Gardell

Judaism and Violence: A Historical Analysis with Insights from Social Psychology
Robert Eisen

A full series listing is available at: www.cambridge.org/ERAV

Printed in the United States
by Baker & Taylor Publisher Services